Textile Surface Decoration
Silk and Velvet

Margo Singer

First published in Great Britain in 2007
A & C Black Publishers Limited
38 Soho Square
London W1D 3HB
www.acblack.com

ISBN-10: 0-7136-6953-5
ISBN-13: 978-07136-6953-4

Published simultaneously in the USA by
University of Pennsylvania Press
3905 Spruce Street
Philadelphia, Pennsylvania 19104-4112

ISBN-10: 0-8122-2000-5
ISBN-13: 978-0-8122-2000-1

Book design by Paula McCann
Cover design by Peter Bailey
Copyedited and proofread by Carol Waters
Project Manager: Susan Kelly
Editorial Assistant: Sophie Page

Printed and bound in China

Contents

Introduction

Silk and velvet have always been thought of as opulent, luxury materials much used by royalty and nobles of many different cultures. Yet today both silk and velvet are accessible and available to us all. Both are treasured for their luxurious lustre, texture and strength, yet are versatile materials that can be decorated in an exciting variety of ways.

We live in a modern ethnically diverse society where we are all used to a wide choice of different traditions, tastes and styles of clothing and personal adornment. The prevalence of makeover programmes on television in the West has influenced the way we see style and design as expressions of individual taste. We are now used to decorating and furnishing our homes with furniture, rugs, artifacts and textiles from many different regions.

Nowadays a broad range of crafts and textile samples from many different cultures are available to us all in museums, craft galleries and shops. Guilds such as the Embroiderers and Quilters and the Feltmakers Association help to maintain strong crafts traditions.

I have selected a range of textile techniques from the simple dyeing and painting of fabric to a range of decorative techniques such as block printing and stencilling and the crafts of appliqué, embroidery and finally mixed media, combining many of these techniques. As far as possible I have tried to present these techniques in their historical and cultural context in order to understand a little about the social and geographical conditions in which these traditions evolved.

I have also selected a number of textile artists using a wide range of techniques in order to inspire the craftsperson or student. Many of these artists have been influenced by the historical traditions and styles of other cultures as well as their own familiar landscapes and personal cultural references. The artists shown in this book mix their materials and techniques to reflect their own creative expression and all use silk and velvet in their work in some way. I would like to thank all those who contributed their encouragement, their ideas and their textile pieces included in the book.

ONE

Silk and velvet

What is silk?

Silk is a luxurious yet natural fibre which can be woven into a fabric that is cool in summer and warm in winter. Silk comes from the filaments of the cocoon of the silkworm. The cultivated silk worm is the *Bombyx Mori* which feeds on the leaves of the mulberry tree. The female silk moth lays more than 500 tiny eggs. The tiny silkworms hatched from these eggs grow until they reach about 10 cm (4 in.) long; then they stop feeding on the mulberry leaves and begin to spin a cocoon. Silkworms will eat a ton of mulberry leaves to produce 12 lb. (5.4 kg) of raw silk. The cocoons are boiled to soften the sericin, a glue like substance produced from the glands of the silk worm. Threads from the cocoons are unravelled and wound onto spools or into skeins of silk. This silk is the colour of ivory.

Hanks and cocoons

Silk is a strong, durable fibre used to produce a very varied range of fabrics. It has strength and elasticity with good crease recovery and feels warm against the skin. Silk comes in a wide variety of finishes and weights. Wild silk, tussah is produced from wild silk cocoons. Silk damask is a self patterned satin weave woven with subtle patterns which emerge as the dominance of either the warp or weft threads change. This type of silk became known as 'damask' after Damascus, the city in Syria, which is possibly where these textiles were first seen by the crusaders.

Silks which are produced and sold today range from lightweight floaty silks – such as chiffon and mousseline – to medium and lightweight smooth glossy silks, such as habutai and the heavier slubbed dupion silks and silk brocades.

Silks including damask

China

In China, sericulture (the production of cultivated silk) has been practised for thousands of years. According to the Chinese, silk originated from the banks of the Yellow River at least 4000 years ago. It is rumoured to have started as an industry in China when the Empress Si Ling Chi learned how to rear the caterpillars on mulberry leaves and unwind silk from cocoons. Chinese silk weavers produced a variety of silk textiles of different styles often featuring the characteristic peony and phoenix motif. In the early days silk was only used by the Emperor and his close relatives at court. Typical of the designs on these imperial robes were the large standing dragons with their paws clutching clouds, hand

embroidered in silk threads onto silk backgrounds. Over the centuries, silk tunics became popular garments with other social classes, and silk itself became a very important part of the Chinese economy.

The techniques of silk production were kept as secret as possible but it is said that in 140BC a Chinese princess smuggled silkworms out of China to Afghanistan, hidden in her headdress. The Silk Road trading which began in 4th century BC had reached its peak by the 5th century AD.

Eventually the breeding of silk worms travelled from China to Japan and then along the 6,000 miles of the Silk Road, with other luxury trade goods, through India to the Middle East and finally to Europe.

Dragon robe

Africa

In Africa silk was traditionally used to make garments for royalty and members of the elite. Silk was also used for the shrouds and shawls worn by the Merina people of Madagascar. Some silks are still produced for the export trade.

Narrow strip weaving is a long standing tradition in some West African countries from a region south of the Sahara, stretching from the Atlantic in the west to Lake Chad in the east. Though much of this cloth is cotton, the Ashanti of Ghana weave *Kente* cloth (a narrow strip silk cloth). *Kente* is a name derived from the Fanti word for 'basket'. These vibrantly coloured woven strips of silk are made into robes; historically this expensive and rare cloth was reserved for royalty, but now it is available to anyone who can afford it.

Kente cloth

Europe

From about the 4th century BC, Roman legions stationed in Syria began to take an interest in the silks they saw there. As its reputation, and eventually the fabric itself, found its way back, Chinese silks became popular in Rome; one Roman Emperor, Heliogabalus (AD 218), wore nothing but silk. In Rome, silk prices were high, but the fabric was much sought after by all classes of people. By AD 500 silkworm farms were beginning to appear in Europe.

English kings and queens and the nobility have worn silk since the 12th century; but the sumptuary laws of Tudor England restricted the dress of the lower classes by forbidding garments of silk, velvet and brocades to all but royalty and the noble classes. As a result, silk was rarely seen by most people. During this period however imported silk thread was used to decorate church vestments and from this emerged the tradition of English embroidery, known as *Opus Anglicanum* (English work), which was highly regarded as fine embroidery throughout Europe.

There had been a small industry in England of silk weaving in ribbons and fringes since the middle of the 15th century. However, in the mid-17th century, following Catholic King Louis XIV's decision to outlaw Protestantism, around 200,000 French Protestants fled abroad from France. Roughly 50,000-80,000 of these settled in London, U.K. Many were from Lyons, the heart of the French silk industry, and they set up silk-weaving businesses in the Spitalfields area of London, using handlooms to weave raw silk imported from Italy. By 1700 Britain was importing silk from Persia and Italy and by the mid-18th century the ships of the East India Company brought Bengal silks back to Britain. Silk became an important industry for areas in the northwest of England, such as Macclesfield, Manchester, Derby and Coventry.

Many attempts were made to cultivate silk in England but the climate was not suited to the raising of silkworms, so silk manufacturers had to import raw and processed silk from the East. From the early part of the 19th century silk manufacturing declined although the silk industry remained strong until about 1860, when the duty on imported French silks was dropped.

Silk was still popular in England throughout the 19th century and was revived further in the late 19th century when Thomas Wardle, the dyer who worked with William Morris, pioneered the dyeing of tussah silk. Wardle imported tussah moths, which had been collected in the wild, and experimented with natural dyes to achieve delicate pastel shades known as 'Art Colours'. At this time, silks were still woven in mills in the Macclesfield area.

Indonesia

In Indonesia, *ikat* silk for garments and scarves is still produced today. The word '*ikat*' comes from a Malay word which means 'tied or bound' and it is a type of weaving that uses tie and dye on either the warp or weft threads before weaving. Silk and silk velvet woven *ikats* have been found all over the world and but are particularly associated with India, Central Asia, Japan, Central and South America, Japan and Africa. They can be found in many archaeological textiles dating back to the 7th century AD. *Ikat* styles vary from country to country and contain designs that have symbolic and ritual meaning. Historically these highly decorative textiles denote the social standing and rank of the noble families who own and wear them.

Ikat dyeing technique

The technique of ikat is to bind or clamp bunches of yarn (often with raffia) before it is dyed to prevent the dye from seeping into the bound areas. There are three types of ikat: Warp ikat, in which the warp threads are bound to form a resist pattern; weft ikat in which the horizontal threads are bound; and double ikat in which both the warp and weft threads are bound.

Producing *ikat* textiles is highly skilled work and requires a great deal of patience as the threads are re-tied many times to get the colour sequences required to achieve the pattern. At each stage, the threads are immersed in a different colour dyebath. The *ikats* are then woven on looms using a weft thread passed across the warp. The resulting patterns are sometimes characterised by their feathery edges. Indonesia produces a variety of woven *ikats* from both fine silk and silk tussah, used for making scarves.

Ikat weaving technique

After the threads have been dyed they are set up on the loom – usually at this stage the warp threads are carefully adjusted to line up with each other. However, weavers in some cultures do not line the threads up precisely, thus producing less accurate patterns with the characteristic feathery edge.

Double *ikats* are woven on a frameless loom where the warp is stretched across the room under tension with the heddles suspended from above. These *ikats* demand a great deal of precision in the weaving, and the resist tying is done finely in two-thread units to create fine detail and fine curves. A sari woven in this manner can take two men up to seven months to complete. Elaborate *ikat* patterns are often handed down from generation to generation in the same family.

There are many decorative elements in the traditional designs of *ikats*. Nature is the main inspiration; mountains, rivers, flowers, plants and birds are often featured, along with crocodiles, lizards and geckos.

Painting colours on warp threads for ikat

India

India has its own ancient tradition of silk weaving and can boast many indigenous silk moths. The country produces several different types of silk: Mulberry; Muga – from moths fed on polyanthus leaves; Tussar – from moths fed on oak leaves; and Eri – from moths fed on caster oil plant leaves. In India, silk is a much-loved fabric and is considered both beautiful and 'pure'. Historically, gold threads were often woven into silk fabrics for clothing, and exquisite carpets were also made from silk.

Traditionally, silk was used for richly decorated saris, furnishings and embroideries, and unique, distinctive styles developed in each area. India became a major exporter of silk and is still the largest producer of silk after China. There are many sari-producing centres, such as Gujerat (which produces Patola silk saris) and Madhya Pradesh (also famous for silk saris). India also produces a wide range of dupattas, caps, turbans and shawls and even quilts made from silk.

In India the Orisson style of *ikat* has a long tradition dating back to at least the 12th century. Weavers migrated there from the Patan area in Gujarat Northern India. Nowadays in Patan, double *ikat* (*Patan Patola*) is still made for traditional saris and ceremonial garments. This original Patola cloth used to be exported to Indonesia for the use of the royal families. These silks were traditionally dyed with vegetable dyes but now some chemical dyes are also used.

Central Asian man's coat warp *ikat* – Collection Jim and Diane Gaffney

Ikat silk scarves

Japan

Japan has a long tradition of producing resist-dyed fabrics and here *ikat*, called *Kasuri*, is also made by binding and dyeing parts of the warp or weft threads before the fabric is woven. *Kasuri* is characteristically woven from silk or cotton, and is traditionally used for kimonos. As in the Indonesian technique described above, the threads are stretched on a frame, selected areas are bound, and then the hanks of thread are immersed in dyepots. For warp *ikats*, the warp threads are bound and dyed, then woven with plain weft threads. More complicated designs are achieved by binding the weft threads precisely, and sometimes the warp threads are painted or printed before the final weaving process. Some *ikats* are made from both warp and weft threads which have been bound to create very distinctive patterns by crossing the resisted areas.

What is velvet?

The origins of velvet are a little obscure; it has existed in the East for centuries, and there are records of silk and linen looped fabrics which date from the 4th century in Egypt. A reference to '500 lengths of velvet' was found in a list of treasures from a Caliph of Baghdad dated AD 809. As it was a luxury fabric, velvet (as well as silk) featured prominently in the portraits of European royalty and nobility during the 16th and 17th centuries. Many portraits of Elizabeth I show her clothed in velvet.

Velvet today is described as 'a luxury fabric with a short dense pile'. It is produced by creating loops in an extra set of warp yarns by inserting narrow rods during weaving. The pile is produced on the loom by the additional third thread and kept in place by the warp and weft. Most velvet is now made by the face-to-face method. The third thread continues across another cloth woven at the same time on the same loom. A fast-moving blade then slices horizontally between the two cloths, separating them. Various types of velvets are produced: voided velvet, in which the pattern with pile only appears in selected places; *cisele* velvet, which contains both cut and uncut areas; and Utrecht velvet, on which the pattern is embossed by etched, heated rollers.

Velvet can be made from a mixture of silk and viscose or from many other fibres such as cotton or linen. It comes in a wide variety of prices, styles and finishes. Silk viscose velvet absorbs the dye well and can be used for a range of fashion and furnishing fabrics.

Italian silk and velvet

Italy is the foremost European country known for the production of velvet. Silk and velvet probably first arrived in Italy from the East, transported by Arab merchants and velvet weavers from Greece, Turkey and Cyprus. By 1247, a velvet weavers' guild was established in Florence; by the end of the 14th century Lucca was also producing velvet as were Venice and Genoa. From the 12th century through to the 18th century, the trade from these cities supplied Europe with sumptuous fabrics which were transformed into a variety of clothing, wall coverings and upholstery.

Venice was a powerful city-state during the Renaissance, and velvet made an important contribution to the ballooning fortunes of Venetian bankers and merchants. Venetian weavers imported silk-moth cocoons from the Orient, Sicily and Spain, and raw silk from Persia and Turkey. The textile industry was well regulated, and emigration was forbidden for textile workers. Both Italy and Spain remained the main European centres of velvet during the 15th and 16th centuries.

Most velvets were traditionally woven from silk, though occasionally European velvets were made with a weft of linen concealed beneath the silk pile; this made the fabric cheaper to produce. As technology developed, patterns could be cut into the pile resulting in voided velvet, and brocaded velvets were developed through the incorporation of gold and silver thread.

TWO

Easy painting and dyeing

Suitable fabrics

There is a wide choice of silks and velvets suitable for painting and dyeing. Generally speaking, the heavier the fabric, the longer dye will take to penetrate the surface; it is necessary to sample each fabric to get the desired effect.

Pongee (Habutai)

This is the easiest type of silk to use for painting. Pongee (habutai) comes in a variety of weights and has a smooth surface. This is useful for scarves as the dyes spread easily across the surface.

Silk satin

This is smooth shiny silk, which is ideal for painting and dyeing. It needs careful washing and preparation to absorb dye well.

Antung

This is a medium weight silk which is often cream rather than white. It is good for painting and dyeing though hard to achieve very strong colours. Heavier and more substantial than habutai it is often suitable for cushion covers or as background for embroidery or *appliqué*.

Dupion

As dupion has an uneven, crisp texture, it is slightly more difficult to paint but dyes well.

Various silks ready for dyeing

Equipment for dyeing silk

Twill

This is an attractive medium-weight silk with a diagonal weave in it.

Crepe de chine, mousseline and chiffon

These very lightweight silks are thin and floaty and make good scarves.

Silk organza

This is very transparent, dyes beautifully and can be used to add to overlay shapes and layers in *appliqué* and embroidery.

Silk velvet

Today velvet which is 82% viscose and 18% silk can be obtained from many suppliers of cloth and though expensive when bought by the metre, is afford-able when bought in larger quantities. Velvet absorbs the dye well and can offer exciting possibilities for the textile designer. In appearance it resembles silk and has the same lustrous surface.

Materials needed:

- There are variously-priced silk dyes, but the simplest are heat-fix dyes which are for use with an iron.
- Silk paints and dyes – Fibre reactive dyes (Procion®), silk heat-fix paints, (Deka® or Pebeo®), acid steam-fix dyes (Dupont®).
- Effect salts – salt crystals.
- Wooden frame – old picture frame or adjustable craft frame.

- Silk pins.
- Rubber gloves – to protect your skin and protective clothing to protect clothes from dye stains.
- Spoons.
- Nose and mouth mask.
- Jam jars – screw top lids for storing dyes.
- Large shallow plastic tray (e.g. cat litter tray).
- Plastic bucket or bowl.
- Soda ash.
- Urea.
- Pipettes or syringes.
- Selection of different sized paint brushes – soft round watercolour paintbrushes or Chinese brushes are best. Decorating brushes and foam applicators can be used to cover large areas with dye.
- Sponges.
- Mixing palettes and water pots.
- Spray bottles of various sizes.
- Masking tape.
- Sheet of plastic to protect the work table.
- Newspapers and kitchen roll.
- Scissors.
- Fixing equipment – iron and hairdryer.
- Fabric pens auto-fade pens or water soluble for marking fabric.
- Markal™ – paint dye sticks.
- Pastel dye sticks.
- Fabric pens/markers.
- Silk/viscose velvet - short pile or long pile (white).
- Silk/viscose velvet - black or other colours.

Health and safety

Before using any of the following methods of dyeing fabric, it is important to think about Health and Safety issues. It is essential treat dyes carefully and according to the manufacturers' instructions, as some of the chemicals may be harmful if used incorrectly. As a general checklist:

- Always protect your hands with stong rubber gloves.
- Protect working surfaces with plastic sheeting or newspaper.
- Wear an overall, apron or old clothes.
- Only use dyeing equipment for dyeing.
- Dry dye powders can be harmful if inhaled – always work in a well-ventilated area.
- Always use a protective mask, which covers your nose and mouth, when mixing dye powders.
- Always read and follow the manufacturers' instructions carefully and exactly.

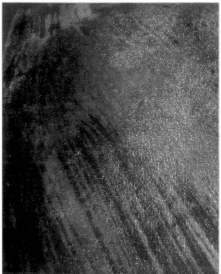

Paint brush marks on velvet

Painted velvet scarves

Preparing fabric

Both silk and velvet will absorb paints and dyes better if first washed in warm water with a gentle soap solution as a scouring agent to remove dressing and gum. Rinse the silk in tepid water and dry before working on it. Be careful not to wring the velvet, which will need to be ironed flat (on the wrong side) before painting. Many of the following dyeing and painting techniques can be used on both silk and velvet but will obviously work differently depending on the surface and thickness of the material. It is essential to do plenty of experiments on small pieces of fabric to get the desired effect.

If you want to dye whole areas of fabric one colour as a background, Dylon™ dyes are the most readily available. They make a large range of colours, which can be used on most fabrics though results are often slightly paler on silk. These are obtainable in most craft shops and hardware stores and there are plenty of leaflets produced by Dylon™ which describe the range of dyes and give instructions on how to use them.

Direct painting

Velvet and silk can be painted directly with a sponge, a foam brush, a large decorators' brush or even syringes (for trickling dye onto fabric). If the velvet is dry when painted, the brush strokes can be quite effective and become part of the decoration. If a softer effect is needed, damp the velvet before painting it and allow plenty of liquid dye to spread across the surface of the velvet blending the different colours and allowing them to merge. Interesting and vibrant effects can be achieved on fabrics by merely dropping the dyes onto the velvet or silk with a plastic dropper then crumpling the fabric up. Derek Williams (below) is an artist who works with silks and acid dyes to create vibrantly coloured examples.

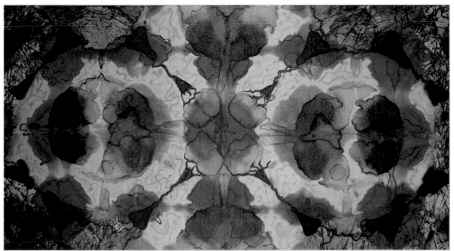

Folded acid dyed silk – Derek Williams

You can also decorate velvets and silks to emulate aspects of the stunning *ikat* method shown earlier (pp.4-5). To achieve this on silk or velvet you need to paint the colours boldly onto a dry surface (don't attempt to blend them). The edges will however spread across the fabric and where they meet another colour will give the blurry effect which is imitative of the *ikat* weaving.

Dyeing and painting larger quantities

Fibre-reactive dyes – Procion MX™ or Dylon™

These dyes work well on both silk and velvet as well as cotton. They come in powder form in plastic containers where they will keep indefinitely. They can be intermixed and also used for screen printing with the addition of Manutex™. You will need to mix them with urea and soda.

Chemical water solution:
• 1 litre warm water
• 140g (5 oz) urea (which helps the dye powder to dissolve and spread evenly)
Dissolve together and put in a screw top plastic or glass jar.

Soda solution:
• 1 litre (35 fl oz) very hot water
• 200g (7 oz) washing soda
Dissolve together and put in a screw-top plastic or glass jar.

These solutions will keep for a long time in airtight jars. To use them to prepare the dyes for painting, follow these instructions:

• Mix a half to one teaspoon of dye with very hot water to make a paste.
• Add 25ml (1 fl oz) of chemical water then 25ml (1 fl oz) of soda solution.
This dye will now be ready to use, but it will only keep for about 4-6 hours after the soda is added. You can use this to paint directly onto silk or velvet.

If you want to prepare your fabric before dyeing it you can use the following recipe:

• Mix 300ml (11 fl oz) soda solution with 1.5 litres (2½ pints) boiling or very hot water.
• Immerse dry fabric for 10 mins.
• Remove and dry fabric.
• Mix 140g (5 oz) urea with 1 litre (35 fl oz) water to make chemical water.
• Mix 1 teaspoon dye in a beaker with a small amount of warm water to make a paste.
• Add 25ml (1 fl oz) chemical water and repeat for each colour.
• Place fabric on plastic sheet. Dye and colour as required.

• Place another plastic sheet over fabric. Roll up and place in a plastic bag.
• Leave for 24 hours, then remove fabric and rinse in cold water until it runs clear.
• Wash in warm soapy water. Allow to dry, then iron gently (on the wrong side if using silk velvet; ironing on the right side will flatten the pile).

To achieve a random dyed effect on silk velvet, use Procion™ dyes in either a plastic or metal bowl, and follow the following recipe. You will need a selection of pipettes to drip the dye onto the velvet.

Method
• Wet the piece of velvet in water and squeeze out very gently so that it is just damp in the bottom of the bowl or bucket.
• Apply dye mix with pipette one colour at a time – either randomly or in a controlled way if preferred.
• When all dye has been used blend the colours together with your hands.
• Tip away excess colour and leave for 30 mins for colours to blend.
• Pour soda solution (1 Tbsp washing soda dissolved in 500 ml hot or boiling water) over velvet to fix the dye.
• Leave the fixative on the velvet for at least an hour.
• Rinse the velvet in cold water.
• Spread the velvet out on plastic sheeting or roll up in plastic clingfilm to fix colour. Leave it for at least 2 hours, but overnight if possible. Then wash the velvet in cold water, until the water runs clear.
• When the fabric is nearly dry, iron on the wrong side to bring up its sheen.

Rapid dyeing in a plastic bag

This is a simple technique which is excellent for dyeing small quantities of silk fabric, cotton, velvet, silk or silk threads. This technique uses less water and more concentrated dye solution.

• Pour 100ml (3½ fl oz) dye mix plus 100ml (3½ fl oz) soda solution into a plastic freezer bag.
• Place the silk or velvet into the bag. Make sure that the material is fully immersed in the dye in the bag.
• Fasten the bag with a tie or elastic band.
• Place in a tray and leave for up to 2 hours.
• Agitate the bag from time to time to make sure that the dye penetrates the silk.
• Rinse and wash out excess dye.

Fixing the dyes

When using Procion™ dyes with silk or velvet, the fabric can be left to dry for at least three hours, or ideally overnight, simply by air drying as the soda solution will have already helped to fix the dyes. When using acid dyes with silk, you will need to fix these by steaming - this can be done in a bamboo steamer, a colander and saucepan, or a stainless steel tiered vegetable steamer. It is often more convenient to use a microwave. If using a steamer, you will need to wrap your fabric up in absorbent paper such as wallpaper lining paper. Roll it up, sealing the ends with tape and securing the roll with string, then place in the steamer. Make sure that it is only lightly steamed and that the water does not come into contact with the roll of material. This is the method usually used for fixing acid dyes.

Acid dyes

Acid dyes give brilliant colour on silk, wool and other protein-based fabrics, and can be set in the microwave or by steaming. You will need to use white vinegar (acetic acid) to drive the dye into the fibres and help to fix it. To make acid dyes, follow these instructions and remember to wear a protective mask:

• Put ½ teaspoon dye powder into a measuring jug and mix with a little warm water. When you have a smooth paste add boiling water to bring the quantity to 300ml (½ pint).
• Pour this into a screw-top jar and store as a stock solution; this solution can be kept for several months.
• Pour 100ml (3½ fl oz) of Procion™ dye mix plus the appropriate soda solution into a polythene freezer bag. Place the silk fabric or threads to be dyed into the bag, making sure the fabric or threads are thoroughly immersed in dye.
Continue with the following instructions:

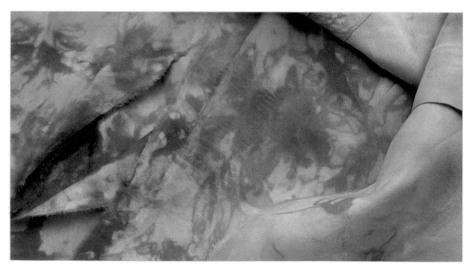

Strips of acid-dyed silks

Microwave colour-fixing

• After placing your fabric or threads in a polythene freezer bag, fasten the top of the bag and place it, upright, in a microwave-proof container. Cover this tightly and securely with clingfilm, but create a few small ventilation holes in the clingfilm to release excess steam.
• Microwave on high for 5 mins and reheat for 2 mins on medium heat.
• Carefully remove the clingfilm, protecting yourself from steam. Wash the threads or fabric in warm soapy water, then rinse until the water runs clear.

Dyeing silk with acid dye

This method is suitable to use with up to about ½ a square metre of silk.
• Always remember to pre-wash your silk using lukewarm water and a few drops of washing-up liquid. Rinse the fabric thoroughly.
• Soak silk in a bowl of warm water (enough to cover the fabric), with approximately 50ml of ascetic acid (white vinegar) mixed in, for a few minutes.
• Lift the silk out of the bowl, and gently squeeze to remove excess liquid.
• Place silk on either polythene/cling film or in small microwavable tray or bowl – arrange the wet silk into interesting shapes, such as valleys and hills.
• Using pipettes or syringes, paint or drizzle the acid dye onto the silk in random patterns. If you want the colours to merge then squeeze the silk together at this stage. If you do not squeeze it, you will achieve a more marbled effect. Remember, the more you handle the silk, the more the colours will blend.
• When you have achieved your desired effect, cover the bowl and microwave the silk (see instructions for 'Microwave colour fixing' above).

Painting on a frame

Velvet can be dyed or painted on a table covered with plastic as it does not need to be stretched over a frame. However, most silk painting works better if you use a wooden frame to stretch the fabric over rather than painting the silk,

Random dyed silk velvets with stencilling

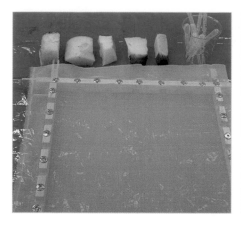

Stretched silk organza on frame

Sponge-painted silk organza

unsecured, on a flat surface. This is especially important if you want to use thin silks such as habutai or silk organdie. Sponges and foam brushes are the easiest tools for creating interesting effects on thin fabrics. The most versatile frames are those which can be adjusted to the size required, but other frames can be used provided the frame surface is flat and smooth and will not snag the silk. When preparing your silk for painting, remember to wash it before ironing to remove any dressing. Set the frame to the size required, then stretch the silk over it and secure the silk using silk pins. Most craft shops sell special claw pins that are specifically designed not to mark the silk. The silk needs to be stretched taut to produce a flat surface on which to paint. Place each pin at approximately 5 cm (2 in.) intervals, keeping the tension as regular as possible. Try to avoid having any areas where the silk is not taut, as the dye will collect here. Adjust and re-position the pins if needed to achieve a tight, even tension. Alternatively you could use double-sided tape along the edge of the frame to hold the silk in place.

You can now paint dye directly onto the silk using brushes or foam pads, which are very absorbent and can be used to paint large surfaces of fabric. A small mixing palette may also be useful. Most craft suppliers will stock several varieties. If you are using silk paints, working with a palette will make it easier to mix the exact shades required. For large backgrounds, mix the dyes in plastic yoghurt pots or glass jars. If you are tracing a design onto the silk from a pattern use either a water-soluble or disappearing pen, or a very soft 4B pencil to trace the lines.

Using syringes

As with velvet, it is not always necessary to stretch silk on a frame unless you are trying to achieve very exact effects. For more interesting random effects, you may want to try using syringes or plastic droppers to just drip or drizzle the dye onto the silk or velvet to achieve some interesting random effects. If this is done in a small plastic bowl it can be microwaved to fix the dye. If you are not using a bowl, remember to protect your work surface with plastic backing before commencing dripping and drizzling.

Steaming

Steaming is a simple way of fixing dyes, as you can use an ordinary vegetable steamer or a pressure cooker. If you use a pressure cooker, wrap your fabric up into a parcel with heavyweight paper secured with string. You can also use a simple tiered steamer or a bamboo steamer. Make sure that you have a good quantity of water in the pan. Steam for up to 15 minutes if you are using small pieces of silk (up to one metre). Allow the silk to cool and then you should be able to wash it gently to make sure that the dye will not run.

For microwave colour-fixing instructions, see page 17.

Spray dyeing

Spray dyeing on silk and velvet is probably the simplest way to create smooth transitions between colours or tones. You can use a variety of techniques to spray dye onto fabrics, from simple toothbrushes or mouth sprays to spray pump bottles (available from craft shops). Probably the easiest method of spraying dye onto fabric is using a toothbrush. This, however, creates a very splattered effect with random spots of dye. It is difficult to direct and can be very messy and of course it takes time to dye a large area of fabric using this method. If you want a smoother dyed effect on either silk or velvet it is best to use another sort of spray.

Mouth sprays are small, inexpensive pieces of equipment which are dipped into the dye (diluted into plastic tubs) then used to blow the dye, through a tube, onto an area of fabric. This can make interesting blends of primary colours

Spray dyed velvet with masking tape   Finished velvet with masking tape removed

but you must always be very careful to spray out rather than sucking in!

Inexpensive small plastic spray bottles can be bought at your local pharmacy and used to spray small areas with dye. These are easy to use and give fairly smooth gradations of colour. Spray tends to work better on velvet, as it is more absorbent, than on silk, on which it tends to produce a more mottled effect. Be aware that these bottles may clog up very easily if the particles of dye are not completely dissolved, so you may need to wash them out frequently, using warm water. Larger pump-spray bottles can also be used; they are useful for covering larger surfaces as they can be pump primed and so do not require quite so much effort.

Air brushes can be used to create a very smooth surface, but these are much more expensive than any of the other sprays.

Remember, when spraying dyes you will need to protect the area around the work as fine spray containing dye can cover surrounding surfaces. You can build up layers of colour by spraying very lightly but take care that any thin silk does not become over saturated or the dye will run.

Using masking tape

If you want to separate areas of colour, try using masking tape or cut or torn paper to resist the dye. This is an effective method when combined with spraying. You can also mask areas with the sticky-back plastic that is sold in a roll for covering schoolbooks. Masking tape is available in art shops, supermarkets and stationers in a variety of widths, and it can be taped over the silk or velvet to make lines, borders or grids. Always make sure that the edges are pressed down firmly so that the dye paste or liquid dye does not sneakily seep underneath.

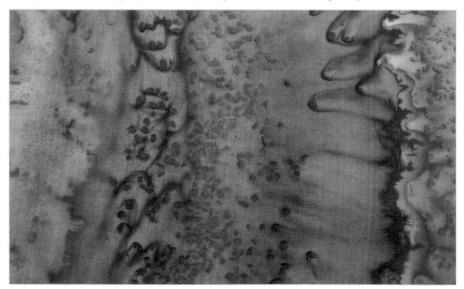

Salt dyed jap silk

Salt-dyed cuffs and band of kimono

When the colours are dry, you re-use the masking tape, re-applying it in a different position to build up interesting and subtle or repetitive designs. Masking tape may be used in straight strips, as it comes off the roll, or torn to make random shapes, or cut into small shapes.

Salt crystal method

Another extremely effective way of creating textured patterns on silk is by using rock salt. Craft shops sell small bags, which you can use to experiment with. When the salt is placed on the wet dye it soaks up the colour to form beautiful patterns. Different salt produces different patterns – common table salt makes a very fine pattern and rock salt crystals create a more defined pattern.

Apply the salt while the dyes on your silk or velvet are wet. Experiment until you get an effect you like; if the fabric is too dry the patterns will not form very well and if it is too wet the salt will become saturated with dye and be unable to form any pattern. If you want to create large areas of bleached out colour, you will need to apply a lot of salt.

Ideally, leave the salt on the surface until the fabric is dry – be careful to remove any salt crystals that are not in the desired place. When you are happy with the pattern, brush off all the crystals before you fix the dye. Finally, wash the silk in warm water to remove any excess salts or dye.

The kimono in the photo above is made from silk antung, a medium-weight silk, and it was dyed in a bucket of navy blue Procion™ dye. The bands on the sleeves and collar were painted with both blue and mauve dyes, then salt crystals were placed on the surface and allowed to dry before being brushed off.

Silk painting using iron-fix dyes

Iron-fix dyes can be used to make more controlled designs and patterns on silk. They are convenient, as they only need to be ironed on the reverse side of the dyed fabric to be fixed, they are acrylic based and they come in a variety of shades from different art and craft shops or specialist mail order suppliers. They are sold in small jars and are designed for painting small areas onto silk, which is usually stretched on a frame.

One of the main iron-fix dyes available is Deka™, which is available in 48 colours. These are dyes rather than paints, so they flow easily. Other good brans include Pebeo™ (29 colours), Setacolour™ (bright luminous colours for painting or dyeing) and Javana™ (51 colours). All these are water soluble and easily inter-mixed. They are usually used with either gutta, which forms a barrier so the paint will not spread over the lines, or in batik with wax acting as the barrier.

All these paints have a low health risk as they contain no solvents or powder and no special precautions need to be taken when working with them. They are very handy for beginners, but cannot be used to cover large areas since they are sold in small quantities.

They can be fixed by ironing on the reverse side for several minutes according to the manufacturer's instructions. Sometimes the product advises you to wait 48 hours before washing and then ironing with a warm iron set at a silk/wool setting. Whatever the instructions, be sure to follow them.

Silk scarves. Joanne Eddon is a textile artist who produces individual hand-painted silk scarves and accessories. Her inspiration comes from Celtic patterns, illuminated manuscripts and the work of artists such as Klimt and Hundertwasser. Her work is painterly, as it shows the brushmarks, and full of vibrant colours.

Silk paints sold in bottles are not recommended, as they are expensive if you want to colour a lot of fabric and they do not have the rich intensity and luminosity of steam-fix dyes.

Resist methods

Gutta

One of the most popular and accessible methods of using a resist on silk is gutta. Gutta is a glue-like substance that comes from certain trees in Malaysia. It is applied to the silk via a plastic pipette bottle or from a tube, to impede the flow of the dye, and it can also be used as an outliner.

Gutta comes in a wide range of colours, from metallics such as gold, silver and copper to black, white and clear gutta. Clear gutta will wash away but other colours are permanent. It is very effective as a resist and if used skilfully can create a soft effect. Use a fabric pen with water soluble ink or a soft pencil (4B) to mark out the design if you want a precise design. Alternatively, if the silk is fairly thin, a design can be placed under the frame as a guide.

Gutta will produce fine lines which will resist different colours of dye painted next to each other. Always allow the gutta to dry before painting in the dye. Make sure that there are no gaps in the gutta outlines or the dye will seep into the areas and 'bleed' over the lines.

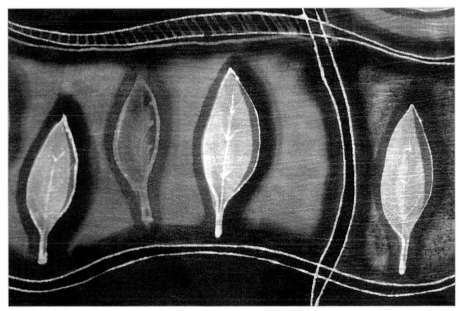

Pink throw. Textile designers Meg Arroll and Winifred Parker use gutta and hand painting in a simple but effective way to produce vibrant silk velvet cushions and throws. They use direct dyes and the gutta is painted onto the reverse of the velvet.

Gutta works very effectively with iron-fix fabric paints as well as dyes. These paints can be diluted with water to achieve a watercolour effect. Remember that your paint will run very quickly over the stretched silk, so do not overload the brush with dye. Ideally use good quality natural hair brushes, including soft round watercolour brushes or Chinese brushes which can give you a good point. Fill the pattern from the centre, allowing the dye to flow out towards the edges. For larger areas, foam brushes are suitable.

Gutta itself is easy and safe to use but does not run as fluidly as hot wax and therefore does not lend itself to especially spontaneous designs. Neither can it be used randomly with a brush to get accidental marks but it is an excellent and versatile medium to use in a classroom situation. If necessary, it can be removed by soaking the cloth in white spirit after the dyes have been fixed.

Making a silk painted cushion

The painted cushion (opposite) was made using Deka™ dyes with gutta as resist. It was inspired by the colours and linear patterns in silk woven *kente* cloth. In Ghana, *kente* cloth was originally woven in narrow strips by the Ashanti and Ewe. Strip weaving has a long tradition in many nomadic tribes, as the narrow strip looms are portable. *Kente* was first woven from silk obtained from unravelled imported cloth in the 18th century. There is a high demand for *kente*, which are now produced in cotton.

Instructions

• Draw out the design, actual size, on paper with a 4B pencil.
• Stretch the silk onto a frame and place it over the paper so that the design is visible through the fabric, to provide a guide for the gutta lines.
• Use clear gutta to outline the design.

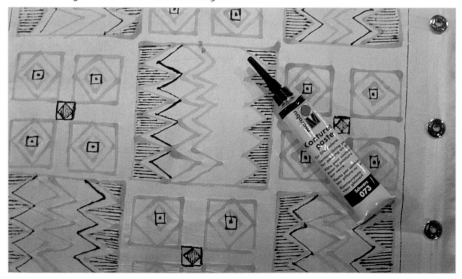

Gutta on jap silk

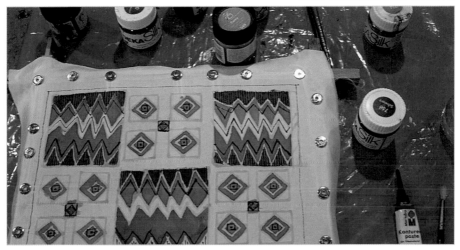

Using Deka™ dyes to paint cushion

• Mix your silk-paint dyes in a plastic palette, to achieve the colours you want. Then paint the design over the gutta.
• When the painted areas are dry, paint black gutta lines over the dyed areas to add extra interest and to create the impression of the woven *kente* cloth.
• To fix both the dyes and the gutta, place a thin cloth (such as lightweight cotton) over the back of the silk and use a hot iron (cotton setting) for 4–5 minutes to fix the colours. Remove the cloth, and gently iron on the back then the surface of the silk.
• Allow 48 hours before you wash the fabric.

For more comprehensive information about Resist Techniques, and step-by-step instructions for each method, see Chapter 3.

Finished painted cushion

Fabric crayons

Pastels and crayons

There is a huge variety of crayons and wax crayons which can be used on fabrics to create interesting effects. These crayons provide softer effects than pens as they can be blended on the surface of the material. Crayons are iron fixed and work particularly well on lighter weights of silk. They can be combined with other techniques; painting backgrounds with dye and then using crayons to highlight specific areas can produce striking results. Wax crayons can be used to create effective textures when rubbed over leaves, bark, lace or string – experiment with a variety of textures.

Textile oil pastels – Markal Paintstiks®

Markal Paintstiks® are real paint in stick form, containing pigment in oil and wax. They can be used on a variety of surfaces and work well on both silk and silk velvet. The paintstiks have a protective film which has to be removed before the colour can be used. This film will reseal itself after use to protect the paint from evaporating. They can be used to draw and the marks can be softened by rubbing with a finger or an old rag to give a more diffused tone.

Paintstiks can be pre-blended on a paper surface or a palette. Colour can be worked into the surface of the fabric with a toothbrush or stencil brush or with the tip of your finger. They work really well if used direct with masks and stencils and when a small amount of paint is rubbed onto a palette a stencil brush can be used to stipple through the stencil to give a soft effect. You can also use

Markal® crayon rubbings

masking tape and build up designs and surface decoration this way.
They come in a broad range of colours with fluorescent, iridescent and pearlised blending sticks which can be mixed with any of the colours to give special finishes. After use the protective outer skin reseals itself keeping the pigment from evaporating. These paintsticks are permanent after 48 hours when the colour is set into the fabric. Finally it should be ironed to fix the colour. The fabric is then machine washable.

Making rubbings on silk and velvet by using Markal Paintstiks®

• Iron fabric ready for the rubbing.
• Select Paintstik colour and cut away skin.
• Place printing block, either a commercially produced printing block or your own block, under the silk.
• Rub Markal Paintstik® over surface of silk. Do not layer it on too thickly.
move block around as desired to overprint if needed with other colours.

NB. Textile pastels are very soft in texture. Like soft pastels they are powdery and can be blended to achieve very subtle effects.

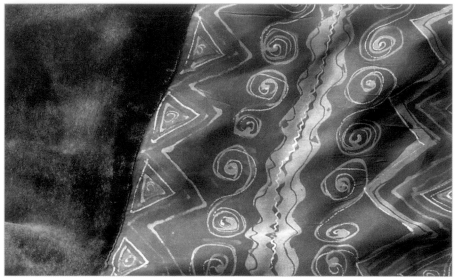

Pink velvet shawl

Pen work

Pens are another effective tool for surface decoration, as they allow you to draw directly onto the surface of the fabric. They work particularly well on smooth silk. The silk panel in the pink velvet shawl (above) was first dyed then painted and finished with a design drawn onto the surface of the silk with fabric felt tip pens.

In India, the traditional technique of drawing elaborate designs directly onto cloth using a fine pen (*kali*) is called *kalamkari*, and it originated in the south-east. The technique is often used to depict narrative scenes, often from Indian mythology. Nowadays this technique is often combined with the use of printing blocks and wax resists. Cloth decorated in this manner came to be known as 'chintz' in England when it was imported in the 17th and 18th centuries.

Felt-tip pens

There are an increasing variety of felt-tip pens made specifically for use on textiles. Dylon™, Setascriband™ and Gonis™ are a few of the popular brands of marker pens widely available in a range of colours. Most are designed to be heat fixed by ironing the decorated fabric on its reverse side once the pen marks have dried. The fabric should usually then be washed 24 hours later, at up to a temperature of 60°C (depending of course on your fabric).

Pens are very versatile as you have a great deal of control with them and they can also be combined with dyeing techniques. Remember though that they should be used for detail and line drawing, or small sections of decoration; they will soon run out if used to 'colour-in' large flat areas. They can be slightly diffused to give a shaded look when dampened by a wash.

THREE

Resist, Devoré and Discharge

For centuries, artists and craftspeople producing textiles have used many inventive ways of decorating or enhancing the surface of cloth in addition to simply dyeing and painting it. Three distinctive methods of decorating textiles to create rich and exciting patterns are *shibori*, *devoré* and discharge.

Shibori

Resist dyeing using tying or stitching is known by different names in different cultures: *shibori* in Japan, *bandhani* in India and often 'tie-and-dye' or 'tie-dye' in the West. These methods can be used to create myriad patterns on silk, velvets and cottons.

The *shibori* culture possibly originated in China but is now associated with Japan, where it dates back at least to the 7th and 8th centuries AD. Traditional Japanese *shibori* covers a variety of ways of manipulating and shaping cloth – often by stitching and securing it – before dyeing it. Areas of the fabric are folded, wrapped, twisted or pleated in particular ways, then the fabric secured with string. Following dyeing, the fabric is untied and spread out to reveal unique and interesting patterns.

Although *shibori* was common in other countries, Japan developed a huge range of techniques such as winding and binding cloth, folding, and clamping techniques, as well as freehand paste resist. *Shibori* was often used to decorate kimono fabrics, such as cottons and lighter weights of silks. Colours and designs were built up by gathering, binding or stitching, then dyeing, then repeating, to achieve exciting intricate patterns. It was not uncommon for a kimono to take a year to complete.

Japanese *shibori* using seeds

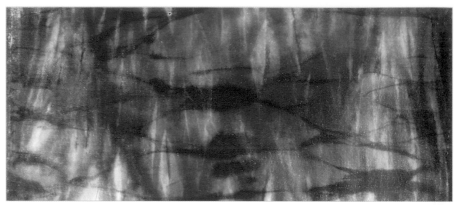

Shibori on velvet

Arashi shibori (bomaki)

Arashi shibori is a newer form of *shibori* which which originated in the 1800s in the Japanese town of Arimatsu. Dyers developed a new *shibori* dyeing technique, which was just as beautiful as the original methods but was much less time consuming. It is also known as *bomaki* which means 'pole-wrapped'. This technique of 'pole wrapping' was traditionally carried out by two men; one formed the intricate pleats while another wrapped the fabric around a very long pole. This technique was named *arashi* meaning 'storm'.

Making an *arashi shibori* velvet scarf

Arashi shibori is suitable for cotton or lighter weights of silk, but can also be very effective on silk viscose velvet. Be creative about the kinds of 'poles' you can use, as there are lots of household options ranging from dowelling, broom handles, or bottles, to tubes made of rolled-up carpet scraps. Your pole should be about 50-60 cm (20 or 24 in.) long, and, if it is made of any porous material, such as cardboard, should be covered in plastic tape, a plastic bag, or plastic clingfilm to

Pole-wrapped silk scarf (twisted)

prevent the dye from seeping away from the fabric. Acid dyes work well with silk to give vibrant colours, but remember to steam-fix them.

Remember, the way you arrange the silk or silk velvet on the pole influences the kind of pattern you will achieve. To mirror the pattern symmetrically, fold the fabric in half so that the pattern and the colour will be the same at both ends.

Instructions

• The whole length of the velvet for the scarf should measure approx. 120/150 x 40 cm (48/60 x 16 in.).
• Immerse your fabric in water, then wring it out until it is damp rather than dripping. Fold the fabric lengthwise, pulling the fabric taut, and twist to form a cord.
• Wrap this twisted cord of fabric around your pole, then fasten it securely at both ends with string. Alternatively, make your fabric into a tube. To do this, measure the diameter of your pole, add about 1.5 cm (⅝ in.) to this measurement to make sure it will fit over the pole, then fold the fabric in half with right sides together. Use your measurement as a guide for the placement of a rough seam, then tack along the long edge to form a tube.
• While still damp, push the scarf-tube onto your pole. When the whole scarf has been rolled down onto the tube push it down firmly so that the fabric bunches up to form tiny pleats. Secure with string.

Tying up string around pole-wrapped scarf. Use a large brush, sponge, or syringes to apply or dribble the dye onto the fabric

• Wearing rubber gloves, use a large brush, sponge or syringes to apply or dribble the dye onto the fabric. Paint the entire scarf with different colours for maximum effect. If you don't want to be left with white areas, make sure that all the little gaps between the pleats are painted. However, you may want the white areas for contrast against the colours in which case leave the pleat-gaps unpainted.

Painting dye on pleated scarf with foam brush. Make sure that the gaps between the pleats are painted unless you want to be left with white areas. This can be an effective way of achieving contrast

• Dry the scarf with a hairdryer or leave it to dry naturally. If acid dyes are used, you will need to steam the scarf to fix them. If you have used Procion, or fibre-reactive dyes such as Dylon™, you may leave the scarf to dry naturally.

This completes the dyeing process. Untie and smooth out your fabric to reveal the patterns you have created.

Detail: *shibori* scarf

Shibori scarf

Silk wrapped around a bottle for dyeing   Detail: *shibori* jacket, Terri Jones

Bottle-wrapping

An empty wine bottle makes an excellent base to wrap silk around.

• For best results, fold a length of jap silk in half, then wrap it diagonally around the bottle and secure it in place with string.

• Place the bottle in a bowl, and apply your chosen dye colours using a sponge. Remember to wear rubber gloves to protect your hands.

• Dry the scarf with a hairdryer or leave it to dry naturally. If acid dyes are used, you will need to steam the silk to fix them. If you have used Procion, or fibre-reactive dyes such as Dylon™, you may leave the scarf to dry naturally.

• After 24 hours, wash your fabric according to the manufacturer's instructions.

Twisting

Using the bottle wrapping technique above, you can also twist your silk before wrapping and dyeing. This will result in a striated pattern when dyed. Follow the instructions for bottle wrapping, but first fold the jap silk in half, then twist it on itself before wrapping around the bottle.

Terri Jones is a textile artist who combines silk dyeing with machine embroidery (see image above right). She has designed a silk antung kimono using very subtle *shibori* in soft blues; the gentle colour contrasts with the delicate machine-embroidered lemon surface decorated with tiny beads.

Potassium permanganate

If you are new to dyeing methods, you should consider experimenting with different fabrics and a single colour or dye to see what varied effects you can produce with simple folding or tying techniques. Potassium permanganate creates an attractive brown colour in various tones on silks, velvets, cottons and linens, and it can be bought in small 25g (1 oz.) tubs from pharmacies. The different fabrics will dye slightly different shades of brown, so it is important to experiment with small pieces if you particularly want to achieve a certain strength of colour. The effects can be quite dramatic if the fabric is folded or scrunched up when put into the dye, so you will need to experiment with different ways of dyeing varied weights of silk. The dye effects are not quite as striking on velvet. Remember, as with all chemicals, this dye must be used with caution – always follow the manufacturer's instructions.

Instructions
• Weigh your dry fabric. Measure out 2.5g (½ teaspoon) of potassium permanganate for each 100g (3½ oz) of dry fabric, and set aside.
• Half fill a large metal saucepan (NB: set aside for dyeing and never to be used for cooking in) with cold water. Heat until boiling.
• Soak your fabrics thoroughly before dyeing, and rinse out.
• Dissolve 2.5g (½ teaspoon) of potassium permanganate (measured out at the beginning) in ½ cup of boiling water. Add this to the saucepan for each 100g (3½ oz) of dry fabric.
• The dye quickly appears as magenta but the finished colour will be brown.
• Simmer your fabric for 2-3 minutes for a light colour or for up to 4 minutes maximum to give a deep, rich brown.
• Remove fabric from the dye, and leave it to dry.
• If you want to discharge this dye you can use lemon juice thickened with Manutex. This discharging method is very powerful, and silk will discharge back to white. For more information on using discharge paste, see pp. 38-9.

Scarf dyed with potassium permanganate

Devoré

The word *devoré* comes from the French verb meaning 'to devour'. *Devoré* patterns on viscose/silk velvet are made using a specially-produced chemical gel which dissolves the cellulose fibres in the velvet, cutting into the fabric to form a pattern and decorative surface effects. The technique is often referred to as 'burnout' and the chemical gel may be applied either by printing or painting. This technique is most effective when used on fabrics made of mixed fibres, in which one fibre is protein (silk) and one is cellulose (viscose). On 18% silk/92% viscose-velvet, the velvet pile is eaten away and the silk gauze remains. It can also be used on velvet with a rayon or cotton pile. *Devoré* on velvet was very popular in 1920s Europe and is still used commercially to produce clothing and scarves.

Contemporary *devoré* using Fibre Etch™

Usage and safety notes

You can create your own *devoré* fabrics from silk-viscose velvet. The easiest way is to use a burn-out gel called Fibre Etch™, which is sold by specialist craft suppliers. Fibre Etch™ is sodium hydrogen sulphate which carbonises the cellulose fibre when heat is applied. The gel or paste is piped onto the fabric through a nozzle; it works by removing only cellulose-based plant fibres – cotton, linen, rayon, hemp and viscose – leaving behind any non-cellulose fibres such as silk or wool. Fibre Etch™ works well on velvet with a viscose pile and a silk backing. Although Fibre Etch™ is not toxic, it can be a strong irritant so always handle it with care and follow the manufacturer's instructions. You must wear gloves and protect your work areas with plastic sheets or newspapers. Always work in a well-ventilated area, and wear a respirator mask with a vapour filter to protect yourself from fumes.

Devoré samples

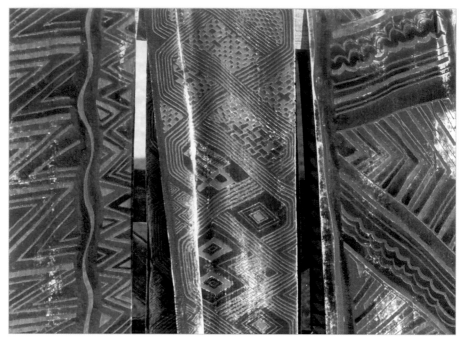

Devoré scarves inspired by Shoowa design, by Caroline Hall.

Caroline is a textile artist who has a workshop and shop in Totnes in Devon. She has travelled extensively and her work is inspired by African designs. The bold patterns she uses rely on overprints to develop the depth and range of colours. Her pattern ideas are developed from her own drawings of plants, and traditional sources such as the African motifs found in Kuba textiles and the decorated doors from Botswana where Caroline used to live. She uses the screen print method of printing the etching medium onto the areas she wants to remove so as to achieve sharp definition.

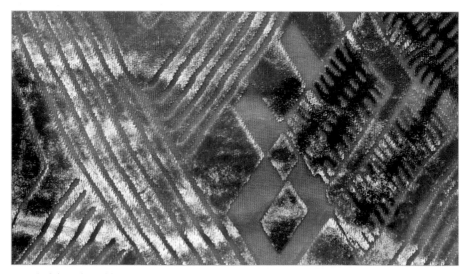

Detail of *devoré* scarf (above)

Instructions for applying Fibre Etch™

• Ideally, use an embroidery frame to stretch the fabric or alternatively, if a large area is needed, place the velvet onto a plastic sheet on the surface of the table.
• The easiest way of applying Fibre Etch™ is through a silk screen – if you have a blank screen you can make a simple design on it with masking tape and print this onto the velvet. This means you can make a repeat pattern, and also ensures that the gel is distributed evenly all over the surface of the velvet.
• Snip the spout of the Fibre Etch™ bottle and apply a thin layer (not raised) of the gel over the pile side of the velvet, drawing on the pattern or design you want the pile to be removed from. Try to avoid any blobs or areas where the gel is applied too heavily; the gel may eat in too far and this can result in holes when the material is ironed. As the silk backing is very delicate, do not leave the Fibre Etch™ on the fabric longer than necessary.
• Make sure that the gel is absorbed well into the fabric – check the back of the velvet to make sure that areas are evenly distributed where you want the design to sit. Dry the fabric thoroughly in a dryer, or with a hairdryer, or leave it to dry naturally.
• Iron on the reverse side of the fabric, using a 'wool' setting. Test the surface of the fabric with a finger to see if the Fibre Etched areas have become brittle. At this stage, it is not unusual for the fabric to look slightly pink. Be careful not to burn your fabric, as this will make unsightly holes in the backing.
• Rinse the fabric under running water, rubbing the pile to allow the fibres to flake off the backing. Wash with liquid soap; allow to dry naturally.

Discharge Technique

Discharge printing and painting is commonly used to produce patterns on silk and velvet. It removes colour from a previously dyed fabric, leaving the colour ranging from off-white to a pale tone. All kinds of velvets can be used to discharge, from silk/viscose to cotton and furnishing velvets.

   Removing colour from fabric, or discharging the dye, is a technique practiced in many parts of the world. The discharge technique is used to make a white or light-coloured pattern emerge from a darker background fabric. In Africa, there is a long tradition of decorating cloth by resist printing by hand, using a starch paste with Adinkra stamps made from calabash. The areas printed then resist the dye. In Nigeria, the Yoruba people use cassava flour paste to produce indigo-dyed *adire* cloth. The resist paste is applied through a metal stencil.

Discharged velvet using *tjap*

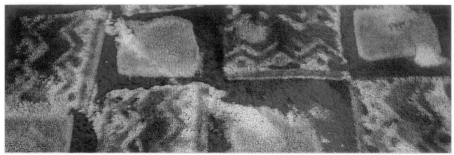

Discharged velvets using wooden blocks

Using discharge paste

This technique can be used to create a variety of patterns and textures on dyed fabrics; the effects you get will depend on the dye originally used on the fabric. Discharge paste is particularly effective on silk viscose velvet and can be applied in a variety of methods including stencilling, block printing, stamping or screen-printing. Most reactive dyes, such as Procion™, are dischargeable. Discharge paste is obtainable from craft suppliers.

Instructions

• Always use rubber gloves and a face mask; these chemicals can be dangerous if not handled carefully.
• If you want to produce a coloured discharge, add a dye to the discharge paste. Otherwise, use the paste as it is.
• Apply the paste to the right side of the velvet, in the design you want the colour removed from.
• If desired, you can combine a discharge method with block printing to achieve repeat patterns. To do this, outline your pattern on a block or rubber stamp, trace over the top of the design with the paste, and stamp the pasted block onto your fabric. Repeat as necessary.
• Once dry, either steam the fabric or iron it with a steam iron on the reverse side. This will actively remove the colour (activate the discharge).
• Once the fabric is dry, wash out any excess paste to reduce any stiffness and dry again.

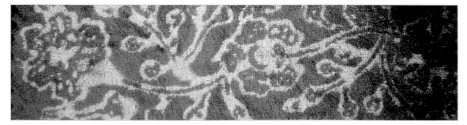

Velvet discharged with *tjap* then overprinted. A *tjap* is a copper printing block used in Indonesia to stamp hot wax onto fabric. You can also paint a bleach solution onto the surface, dabbing it on with a large paintbrush or sponge, then use the block to stamp bleach onto the fabric's surface to discharge the dye.

Discharged velvet stamped with bleach

Using bleach

Household bleach will remove the colour from a variety of fabrics, but if you are not careful it can easily cause damage in the same way as acid does. If you do use bleach, it is important to experiment with different dilutions; if used too strong bleach will destroy fabric, especially thin silk. Household bleach gives uneven results where the amount of colour discharged will vary depending on the strength of the bleach. Commercially dyed fabrics do not always discharge effectively. You can achieve an 'antique' effect where the colour is only partly discharged.

Instructions

• Bleach must be treated with caution as it is a hazardous chemical. It is best to wear a mask (ideally one with a vapour filter) when working with bleach. Always work carefully in a well-ventilated room and keep bleach away from eyes and skin as they can be severely irritated. Always wear rubber gloves and cover all surfaces with protective plastic sheeting. Remember to keep chemicals such as bleach in tightly-sealed, clearly marked containers, well out of the reach of children or pets.
• First, experiment with different strengths of bleach dilution, beginning with about one tablespoon of household bleach to three tablespoons of water and varying your measurements from there, until you get the results you want.
• If discharging velvet, lay the fabric pile-side up on plastic sheeting.
• Pour household bleach into a small beaker and dilute as/if necessary. For maximum effect use undiluted bleach, provided you have already tested it on a scrap of your chosen fabric to make sure it will not destroy the fabric.
• Apply bleach (or bleach dilution) with a small paintbrush or fill a plastic bottle with a nozzle and use it to draw directly onto the fabric. Remember that bleach will spread out on the surface of the fabric so the design will be slightly broader than the lines you draw. It can also be patchy at times. However, this can add random and interesting effects. Once the bleach is dry, use a steam iron lightly on the back of the fabric to activate the discharge. Do not overdo this process or the fabric will burn.
• Neutralise the fabric to prevent rotting. Add approximately 50 ml of vinegar to one bucket of cold water, and soak the fabric in this for at least 10 minutes.
• Rinse, wash, and dry the fabric as appropriate.

Experimenting with discharge methods

If you are interested in the discharge technique, you might like to try some of these suggestions to achieve different effects:

• Try discharging black velvet – the discharged areas often turn a rusty reddish brown.
• Splatter or sponge bleach (or bleach dilution) onto the surface of your fabric to create random mottling.
• You can achieve an antiqued and faded effect by applying bleach or paste unevenly with a stamping block; the strength of each motif will vary with the amount of bleach applied to the surface and the pressure applied to the block.
• Discharging can be combined with many other surface techniques, such as stencilling. Apply discharge through a stencil or onto a block, then use the same stencil or block to print your fabric with a repeat pattern.
• If using Procion™ or cold-water dyes you will only need to iron the fabric to fix the colour. If using acid dyes, you should neutralise them with vinegar after dyeing.

Winifred Parker uses discharge by screenprinting onto a special black dischargeable velvet to produce interesting designs taken from her sketches of moving figures. Here the colour is thoroughly bleached out giving definition to the white areas.

• If you want to use discharge on natural fabrics, you may want to try using commercial discharge paste; it is not as strong as bleach, although it does smell strong. It is sold in 225 g (8oz) jars. The paste is usually white and can be applied using an applicator bottle, brushed on with a firm brush, or used to print designs from blocks or stamps (see Chapter 4). It is also the right consistency to use for screenprinting. If you are using thinner silks this is probably the best medium, as overuse of bleach could rot the fabric.

• If you would rather use discharge paste or bleach for screenprinting, add a thickening agent called Manutex® to the paste or bleach to achieve an effective consistency.

• Try adding colour, such as *Lumiere* dyes or Jacquard fabric paints, to the bleach or discharge paste. These are concentrated pigment colours that remain unaffected by the bleaching action of the discharge paste. After the fabric is discharged using these colours, it should be fixed by steaming for up to 15 minutes. Acid-dyed fabrics should be neutralised before fixing, by soaking them in a bucket of cold water with approximately 50 ml of vinegar added, for at least 10 minutes. Fibre-reactive dyes need only be air-dried before fixing.

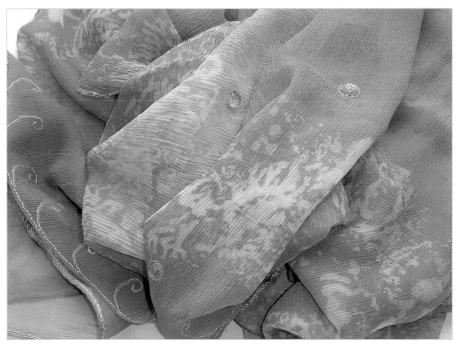

Diana Shone specialises in producing fine discharged and embroidered silk mouselline scarves and throws. Her designs are inspired by the soft colours of the English countryside. She paints the silk loosely in soft colours and spreads the discharge randomly onto the surface of a plastic sheet. She then compresses the silk between this sheet and another, and the feathery pattern emerges. Diana then goes on to produce exquisite scarves, finely embroidered at the edges (see Chapter 5) in a style inspired by the edges of saris and Indian scarves.

FOUR

Blockprinting and Stencilling

Blockprinting and stencilling are effective techniques for combining with the sumptuous and light reflecting qualities of silk and velvet; the inks or dyes used lie on the surface of these fabrics enhancing the contrast between the light reflective surface and the dull pigment of the printing medium. Sometimes these effects almost seem to be three dimensional, appearing to etch the surface, particularly when using velvet.

History: *different cultural traditions*

Japan

Japan has a long tradition of dyeing, painting and printing fabrics for kimonos and robes. In the Nara period, *kokechi* (tie-dyeing), *rokechi* (wax-resist dyeing) and *kyokechi* (block-resist dyeing) were all recognised techniques. The Japanese word *kata-zome* includes both stencil-dyeing and printing from blocks. However, stencil-dyeing became easier when wooden stencils were replaced with stencils made of thick paper. Sophisticated stencil-cutting developed, and small delicate designs became possible. During the Edo period, these techniques developed even further, and stencils, paste resist and hand painting were used to produce pictorial designs.

Indian woodblocks

India

India has a vibrant tradition of block printing (often using indigo), which dates back many centuries. Traditional techniques are still used today. Indian textiles have been exported since the 15th century; today the main textiles centres are Gujerat, Rajesthan and Andra Pradesh, where blockprinting workshops still produce fabrics dyed with vegetable and chemical dyes for clothing, furnishing and fashion exports.

The wooden printing blocks used are made by skilled craftsmen from seasoned teak wood. The block-maker carves the design out of the underside of the block and makes a wooden handle for the back. The block is drilled with two or three holes to allow the passage of air and to release excess printing paste. The printing is done from left to right, using colour that is evened out in a tray. Blocks are designed for different functions: they indicate where the material should be tied for tie-dye; they create guidelines for embroidery; or they are simply used to print directly onto the fabrics.

Indian wooden blocks can often be purchased from craft suppliers and sometimes from shops that import furniture and other artefacts from India. They can be used in a variety of ways, for either printing with fabric dyes or with bleach or discharge paste. The patterns are often intricate and frequently designed to make borders for saris or other clothing.

Africa

In Africa, cloth has been printed and dyed for centuries. Often motifs are stamped with calabash stamps, using starch paste as a resist. The cloth is then dyed, usually with indigo. The two main examples of African printing are the *adinkra* cloths of Ghana and the *bokolanfini* (mud cloths) of Mali.

Calabash printing samples

Calabash-stamped cloth

Adinkra is a printed or stamped cloth which has a long tradition in Ghana. This cloth is associated with royalty, having been worn by several kings, and the symbolic motifs have been handed down for generations. These symbols convey specific meanings and between 50-70 designs are still commonly used. Originally the cloth was only worn for funerals but now is worn for other celebrations including white *adinkra* for weddings.

These *adinkra* cloths are stamped using a calabash, which is a type of gourd. The calabash is tied to a handle of bamboo sticks and is very lightweight. The stamps are slightly curved so that the dye can be put on with a rocking motion. The cloth is stretched flat and divided into sections. The symbols are then printed onto the sections, the printers choosing designs and stamps that convey specific messages. No two cloths are ever alike. Traditionally the dye came from the bark of the badie tree but now synthetic dyes are used. Simple, modern versions of *adinkra* cloth are now printed for the tourist market and these are made using foam blocks rather than the more delicate calabash stamps.

The Bambara people of Mali produce *bokolanfini* (mud cloth), which is decorated by the women. The cloth is coarse cotton and was traditionally grown, spun, woven and decorated in the same villages.

The cloth is first soaked in a brown solution, made from pounded leaves,

Markal™ crayon rubbings and block printed silk scarf

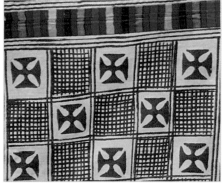

Bokolanfini cloth

until it turns a deep yellow colour; then is decorated with the mud. The mud is taken from deep ponds and then fermented in a pot for about one year; during this time it turns completely black.

Bamboo and metal spatulas are used to draw designs onto the cloth, which is spread on the floor. Designs are then outlined using a wider tool, mud is spread over the remaining areas. This design stage can take weeks to complete.

Finally, a caustic soda solution is painted over the yellow areas to bleach them white, and the cloth is left out in the sun for a week to complete the bleaching process. The designs produced are simple abstract and geometric with symbolic meanings. Many cloths are made to order; specific patterns and motifs are requested by the buyer.

Europe

Blockprinted fabrics from Durham, England, have been dated back to as early as 1104. They have also been found in Italy dating back to the 13th century and in France from as early as 543 AD. Blockprinting was certainly carried out in German monasteries in the Rhineland between the 10th and 14th centuries, when it was used to decorate roughly-woven garments and hangings. Blockprinting was a simple method of producing surface design and was not a suitable method for producing really fine designs. Between the 10th and 14th centuries, blockprinting workshops were also established in Holland, Germany, France, Switzerland, Portugal and England. During this time, the cloth used was mainly linen but samples of silk have also been found.

Early blocks were made of walnut or pear wood. The patterns used were quite simple and they were printed by stamping small wooden blocks repeatedly onto a plain background fabric. Typical examples of early designs in the medieval period consist of a single or paired animals enclosed in circular shapes, and some surviving examples from the 12th to the 14th centuries depict flat patterns of heraldic animals and birds.

In the 14th century figure scenes began to appear, printed using larger blocks. Designs became more elaborate, incorporating animals and birds with monsters, as well as architectural and floral designs.

Italy

By the 14th century, Italy had established itself as a major centre for silk weaving. Large quantities of raw silk, patterned silks and velvets were imported from Georgia, Persia and Syria, and the Orient. Venice established important trade links with the East and the influence of different techniques and designs spread. By this time, many fabrics were being printed with gum, then gold and silver leaf metals were impressed on the shapes. There is evidence of a recipe from an Italian master dyer who describes how to decorate cloth using a wooden block.

In the early 15th century, the artist Cennini mentioned blockprinting in his treatise on painting. He recommended that black designs should be printed onto red, yellow, blue or green cloth, with the details painted on using a brush. The printers of cloth belonged to the same guilds as painters, and they were regarded as inferior to weavers because the designs used were derived from woven textiles. During this time the 'pomegranate' motif, which originated in the East, became a popular design on Italian silks and velvets.

By the mid-1500s Venice was an important centre for the production of velvet. Woven velvets were produced with large floral patterns that included pomegranates or pine cones and flowers. They combined gold and silver threads with silk pile and perfected the *alto basso* technique – woven velvet cut in two or three heights of pile to create a relief effect.

Detail of gold-printed silk velvet fabric with Venetian and Florentine pomegranate motifs produced by Mariano Fortuny. During the early 20th century, printing on silk and velvet became fashionable again as techniques were revived by Mariano Fortuny, a Spanish designer who lived in Venice from 1871-1949. He had acquired a large collection of antique silk and velvet fabrics from the 15th, 16th and 17th centuries and he based many of his own designs on these fabrics. Fortuny created gold, silver and metallic block-printed and stencilled silks and velvets that echoed the designs and look of these antique fabrics, and his work was further influenced by Byzantine, Persian and Islamic silks. Fortuny pleated dyed silk so it would sculpt the wearer's body; this effect was extremely fashionable between 1910 and the 1920s.

Britain: developing printing techniques

Roller printing was developed in the late 19th century. Vegetable dyes, which had been used for centuries, were superseded by the cruder colours of the new aniline dyes discovered by Perkin in 1856 from the distillation of coal tars.

William Morris revived the craft of block printing in the latter part of the 19th century, using vegetable dyes with hand blockprinting. In 1881, he established a print works at Merton Abbey on the banks of the river Wandle near Morden in Surrey. Here he used the river for madder dyeing, established a dye house and had pits dug for indigo dyeing. Morris learned dyeing techniques by studying 16th- and 17th-century herbals and dyeing manuals. He also developed the indigo-discharge technique with Thomas Wardle at his dye works in Leek. Wardle had travelled extensively in India and this experience influenced his design work as well as the types of silk he used. Wardle worked closely with Morris in producing dyed silk threads for embroidery and yarns for woven textiles and velvets. Using indigo-discharged fabrics, Morris created many furnishing fabrics inspired by English gardens, orchards and his love of medieval art.

Getting started - simple printing

Blockprinting or printing with stamps is an easy and economical way of printing fabric. A slight variation and unevenness in colour is characteristic of blockprinting; this occurs when printing, depending on the pressure used and amount of printing paste on the block.

Printing on fabric can be very simple; at the most basic level, you can use any object that makes a mark, from leaves, cotton reels, pieces of sponge, card or string to any small items that have an interesting surface or shape, dipped in paints thick enough for printing. Printing blocks can also be made from a selection of materials such as rubber, foam, card, string and lino. Many craft shops now sell a large variety of small wooden blocks and rubber stamping

Wooden and corrugated card blocks

Calabash foam printing on velvet

blocks. There are a variety of cheap, all-purpose, acrylic-based paints you can use for experimenting with textures and patterns before you start work with more expensive fabric paints.

As silk and velvet are expensive fabrics to work with it is useful to have an idea how your print will look before you commit yourself to working on fabric. Experiment with trying out the designs on different papers. If you get a soft subtle effect you can enhance this by adding some painted marks.

Experiment with different textured items, such as crushed foil, or pebbles, by glueing them to the surface of a block. Glue string to card blocks using Marvin medium, positioning the string carefully to build up interesting textured designs. Corrugated cardboard cut into pieces and mounted onto a cotton reel or a cork from a wine bottle makes another useful block. Effective simple patterns can be printed directly onto silk or velvet, varying the amount of paint that you use to get different effects.

Calabash and foam blocks

Sponges

Sponges are useful for applying printing paste to the surface of your blocks and they can also be used to print very simple but effective patterns on any fabric.

Foam blocks

Sheets of foam in various thicknesses can be obtained from most craft suppliers, and easily cut into shapes and designs to print with. Foam blocks can also be made directly from other printing blocks.

Instructions

• Draw the shape you want to make into a block onto a piece of paper or card. This shape can be anything, influenced by natural patterns (leaves, stars, clouds, etc) to motifs, figures, symbols, or other stamps or blocks you have seen. Be creative. Cut the shape out, to make a paper or card template, and place it on the surface of the foam or polystyrene.
• Transfer this shape by drawing round the outline. Then cut out the shape using scissors or a craft knife, taking care to control your scissors or craft knife especially if cutting out rounded shapes or curves.
• Glue this piece of cut foam onto either another layer of foam or something more solid, such as a piece of card or wood. Make sure that the block will be easy to hold, press and lift away from the back. If necessary, attach a small makeshift handle, made from card, using glue or tape.
• Printing paste can be applied to foam blocks using a roller, or by stamping the block into a thin layer of printing paste in a tray. Be careful not to soak up too much colour on your block, unless this is an effect you are aiming for.

Foam block motifs from Turkish rug

Polystyrene blocks

Polystyrene blocks can also be used to print onto fabric (even the polystyrene used as packaging for pizza bases can make an effective printing block). As the surface is soft, you can easily etch desgins into it using a ballpoint pen or even a sharp pencil. To cut shaped blocks, follow the instructions for 'Foam blocks' above. Printing paste can be applied to polystyrene blocks using a roller.

Wooden blocks

Traditional wooden printing blocks are no larger than 30cms (12 in.) square; anything bigger would be difficult to print with. Small commercial wood blocks are sold at craft shops and decorating outlets; they come in a wide choice of designs. Often museum shops are a good source for small traditional Indian woodblocks. Wooden blocks are much better than foam or polystyrene blocks for printing more intricate or delicate designs onto fabric. They can be used with discharge paste and overprinted.

Rubber stamps

These are sold at most craft suppliers and are available in an increasing variety of sizes and patterns. The more intricate stamps are often sold in strips, so that they can be cut up as required and mounted onto foam. They can be overprinted and make good printed strip patterns.

Rubber stamps printed on velvet   Contemporary rubber blocks

Softsculpt™

Another way to create your own unique blocks is to use a material such as Softsculpt™, which can be impressed with a design and mounted on a block. This thermoplastic foam is sold in sheet form, and it can be used to make a negative design of a particular woodblock or texture.

Instructions
• Heat an iron and place the Softsculpt™ between two layers of baking parchment.
• Set the iron to its wool/cotton setting and run it over the parchment-covered Softsculpt™ for about 60 seconds.
• Still covered in the baking parchment, press the Softsculpt™ firmly onto the raised surface pattern you wish to replicate. This could be, for example, another woodblock, an object such as a brooch, or indeed any textured surface. Press the object and the Softsculpt™ together for about ten seconds.
• Pull them apart gently. Leave to cool. The Softsculpt™ will now have the pattern embossed on it and, when cooled and separated from the parchment, can be used for printing.

Other equipment

As well as your printing blocks, you will also need the following:
• Plastic containers for printing paste - margarine tubs or similar are good for this. You can label them and use them for the same colours again.
• Containers for storing your printing blocks after use.
• An apron, gloves, etc to protect your skin and clothes.
• Foam, or a brush, to apply printing paste to smaller blocks.
• Rollers designed for lino printing. Useful for applying printing paste to the surface of large blocks, and also for rolling over the back of thin, flat blocks to apply even pressure when printing.

Remember, block printing can be used to embellish embroideries and appliqués or mixed with other textile techniques. It can be combined with other methods, such as rubbings with Markal™ crayons, to create varied, unique and interesting surfaces. Be creative and don't be afraid to experiment with different combinations of methods and techniques.

Block printed embroidered square

Lino printing

Lino can be used to print effectively onto fabric and paper. Linoleum was invented in 1860 by Frederick Walton as a waterproof floor covering. The name comes from the Latin *linum* ('flax') and *oleum* ('oil'). Lino is made from ground cork and resins combined with linseed oil and finished with a waterproof surface. Lino for craft purposes can be bought from specialist craft shops. Lino cuts are made by gouging out parts of the linoleum, then inking the surface and printing from the block.

Lino can be used to produce a range of types of work, from very pictorial to simply texturally decorative. The advantage of lino is that it is very durable and can be re-used repeatedly. However, printing with lino is a slow and laborious method, so is best used when you want to print a repeat design over a large surface, such as a length of fabric to be made into clothing or furnishings.

Equipment needed:
• Lino blocks. These can be obtained from major craft shops and suppliers. They come in a range of sizes, from 15 x 10 cm (6 x 4 in.) upwards.
• Lino cutting tools. Often these are sold as a set with a wooden handle and a variety of different cutting blades.
• Rollers, to ink up the surface of the lino or wood block.
• Sheet of thick glass on which to spread the printing paste.
• Printing paste – this could be a mixture of textile dye with a thickener added or ready-to-use textile paint sold in plastic containers, purchased from craft suppliers.
• Discharge paste. Add dye to this if a colour is needed.
• Wooden block, if you want to mount your lino to make it easier to handle.

Transfer your designs to the surface of the lino by placing carbon paper under your original drawing and tracing over it. If the design is relatively simple, or you are confident, you might want to draw freehand onto the block. To prepare the block for printing, rub the surface with fine sandpaper to help the ink adhere.

Lino block and squares

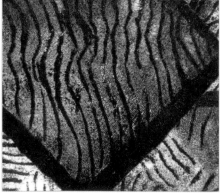

Lino printed squares

Glass or acrylic sheet paint print

Another way to print fabric is by using sheets of glass or acrylic to apply the base colour. A4 (210 x 297 mm [8 x 12 in.]) acrylic sheets can be obtained from most glass suppliers. When you are just starting out, use acrylic paints to experiment with – this method uses up a lot of printing paste.

Instructions:
• Decide on your final design, sketch it out or if you are copying another pattern, make sure you have your reference handy.
• Use a roller to coat the glass or acrylic sheet in printing paste. Roll it out over the whole surface of the sheet.
• Using a comb, stick, blunt pencil or a piece of cardboard to 'draw', remove the printing paste to reveal your pattern or design.
• Carefully place fabric (or paper for your test piece) face down onto the glass or acrylic sheet in one even movement.
• Use a clean roller to press gently over the back of your fabric.
• Slowly and evenly 'unpeel' your fabric from the sheet, revealing your printed design. Lay the fabric on a flat surface to dry.

Stencilling

Decorative stencilling on cloth has a long history in many cultures of the world. Stencils produce a positive or negative image. Dye or paint is applied through the cut areas, or around the outside of a shape, to decorate the fabric. The subtlety of stencilling comes from varying the pressure applied or the amount of dye used. Stencils can also be used with a resist to produce a negative image on the fabric, which can be dyed at a later date.

Japan

Stencilling has traditionally been very popular in Japan. Silk threads or strands of hair glued in several directions, like a net, were sandwiched between two sheets of waterproofed mulberry fibre paper. The hairs and threads reinforced and strengthened the stencil so that, when the patterns were cut out with a long thin knife, the paper did not fall apart. The Japanese refined the use of stencil bars to the extent that eventually only ties of human hair or silk were used. These ties were so fine that they were almost invisible and yet were very strong and able to hold floating shapes in place.

West Africa

In Nigeria, the Yoruba people traditionally used a starch paste made from cassava root flour and water to act as a resist when the fabric is dyed. This starch paste is often applied through a metal stencil, sometimes cut from corrugated roofing tiles that have been hammered flat. Designs are then marked out and cut with a chisel. The stencil design is repeated all over the

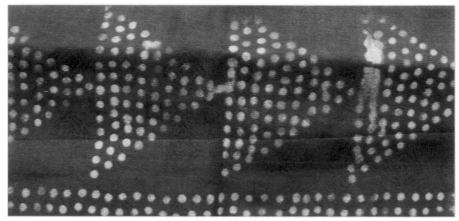

Indigo dyed paste resist West Africa

cloth. There have been many famous stencilled cloths; some are called *Oloba*. There is an *Oloba* collection now in the British Museum.

Cut your own stencil

You can cut your own individual stencils from a variety of different materials; it is simplest to use paper, since this can be either torn or cut with scissors. If you want more precision, you can cut your stencil from the type of acetate sheets used for overhead projector transparencies. These can be bought from most stationers. Because they are transparent, acetates are the ideal solution as they make it easy to see where the stencil should be positioned.

Equipment:
• A good craft knife. The safest are those with retractable blades.
• A cutting board or a strong piece of card.
• A piece of acetate or transparent plastic or stencil paper (available from craft suppliers).
• Tape for fixing the stencil in place – ideally use low-tack tape so that the stencil does not get sticky.
• A design to use for the stencil. The design must be drawn boldly enough so that you can see it through the stencil. Use a photocopier to reduce or enlarge the design until it is the size you want.

Instructions
• Tape the edges of your design securely to a flat cutting surface.
• Tape the acetate stencil on top of the design. Ideally you should leave a clear border of about 2–3 cm (¾–1 in.) around the whole design to prevent dye or fabric paint overflowing the edges when you are dyeing. It will also make the design stronger if you are cutting large shapes out of the stencil.
• Cut round the design with a sharp knife or hot stencil knife. If using a craft

Laser-cut stencils

knife, begin by cutting the longest edges, as these are easier to cut than more intricate, curved lines. Press down on the stencil firmly and cut smoothly right through the surface of the acetate. It may help to turn the acetate round to make the angle easier to cut. Remember to keep your fingers well away from the blade of the knife.

• Once you have cut out the whole design, make sure that all the small shapes are fully cut out. If you have any large interesting shapes left you may want to use these to make another stencil.

• You can alter the look of the stencilled sample by varying the colour of the dye background before stencilling. An effective way of doing this is by spraying the surface of the fabric first.

Positioning the stencil

• Mask off the area in which you want to position a stencil.

• If possible, draw guideline marks in water-soluble pen.

• Secure the stencil with a piece of masking tape in each corner (check first that it will not damage the fabric, by testing a small piece of masking tape on the surface of the material).

Preparing to paint

- Place fabric paint in a saucer or into a plastic container – empty margarine tubs or yoghurt pots are ideal.
- Use either a stencil brush (a flat-ended brush) or a sponge. Dab tip of brush or sponge onto a piece of paper to offload excess paint. Keep a paper towel handy to blot off any excess paint as you continue, dabbing onto the surface of the fabric as necessary.

Medieval tile acetate cut stencil, with a sponge

- Remember not to put too much paint onto the stencil, as runs of colour will form underneath. You can always build up to the colour-effect you want with several applications of colour, but it is much more difficult to remove paint once the damage has been done.
- Sponges work well for painting, and you can cut a large synthetic sponge into any size that you need.

Applying the paint

You can work with just a single colour at a time, or you may want to try a mixture of colours to experiment with blending. Use a separate brush or sponge for every colour. If using a brush, hold it upright so that the flat end hits the stencil in a stabbing motion – the end of the brush must not be applied at an angle. Hold the stencil firmly so that your design will be crisp and accurate. Remember to leave the stencil in place until the paint is dry, to avoid smearing.

Shading

Shading can be used to give your design more illusion of depth.

- Apply the first coat of fabric paint.
- Allow it to dry naturally or heat-fix it with an iron.
- Using a slightly different shade of paint, stab the brush or sponge over the edge of the design or wherever shading is required.

Removing the stencil

- When all the paint is dry, slowly remove the stencil and wipe the back.
- Carefully put the stencil to one side, on a piece of clean paper, until it is completely dry. Clean it, and store it flat to use again.
- If necessary, touch up any blemishes using an artist's fine paintbrush.

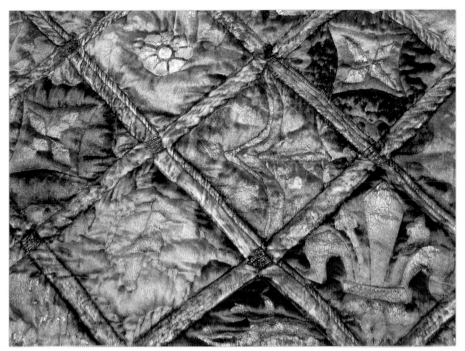

Medieval-tiles quilt. The surface was designed to give an antiqued, aged look, which reflected the worn surface of the original tiles that provided the inspiration for this design. Each square was stencilled with a sponge and various metallic fabric dyes, and each 'tile' was treated individually. The pressure of the printing sponge was varied from one tile to another. Some areas were also lightly foiled to give an added glisten and sheen.

Stencilled and spray-dyed velvet bag. A laser-cut stencil was used with metallic gold print paste. This was left to dry, and then a purple dye was sprayed over the motif. The gold print paste resisted the purple, although it was effective on the surrounding surface. This created a stronger contrast.

Experimenting

Like blockprinting, stencilling is a versatile method. Experiment with stencilling on different surfaces and fabrics, and with combining stencilling with other techniques.

Try some of these suggestions to develop your own designs:

• Overprint with different shades or tones of colour, or use a combination of matt fabric paints and metallic paints.
• Using only selected parts of the stencil, place the stencil on the design where you want to print and apply the colour with a light feathering motion. If using a brush or sponge, you can control how much of the stencil is printed onto the fabric.
• To achieve an antique, worn effect use only the very lightest of touches.
• Use several different colours of stencil paint on the same design at the same time. Often gold, silver and bronze, for example, look good together. For a more dramatic effect, you could experiment with contrasting complementary colours.
• Try using wooden and rubber blocks with foam blocks and stencils, and combine these techniques with various others including stitching, quilting, collaging or foiling.

Printed and discharged velvet bolster cushion. Combining the two techniques of block printing and a discharge method on velvet can result in a subtle antiqued effect; the decoration of this velvet cushion was based on designs and motifs from a Turkish rug.

Project notes

The silk velvet jacket (details below) was inspired by the silk velvet coats designed by Mariano Fortuny (see also p.46); he used various techniques such as block printing over areas of discharged velvet to create the effects of an antique textile. The motif was printed with a lino block, and is adapted from motifs on Italian textiles of the 15th and 16th centuries. These were the main influences on Fortuny's printed velvets.

The fabric was first painted in both navy blue and crimson cold-water dyes, using large foam brushes and allowing the colours to merge into one another in places. Dyes were painted onto dry silk/viscose velvet, which had been laid out on a large table covered in plastic sheeting. The sleeves were painted separately in purple, and the collar in crimson. The front and back of the jacket were discharged with bleach; this was sponged directly onto a wooden printing block, which was then pressed down on the front and back panels. The fabric was wrapped up in large plastic bags to help set the dye and it was then allowed to dry naturally. When the sections of the jacket were dry, the areas that had been discharged were over-printed with a light gold printing paste to give a very subtle antique effect.

Block-printed, Fortuny-inspired velvet jacket (details)

FIVE

Embroidery

This chapter concentrates on a small number of hand embroidery stitches popular in different parts of the world. Hand embroidery requires little equipment and is portable; you can work almost anywhere and pick it up at any time. It is an easy and accessible way to produce unique designs. Only basic equipment is required: a small pair of sharp embroidery scissors; needles; a thimble; and fine steel pins. Craft suppliers sell useful small transparent plastic boxes for storing your threads and other small (easily lost) bits and pieces.

Hand embroidery traditions

China

For traditional Chinese embroidery, silk thread was either twisted, to give a more subdued finish, or used as silk floss. Only a few different stitches were used: stem stitch for outlines; straight stitch, often to denote leaves and flowers; Chinese knots; and couched thread. Generally, satin stitch was used to cover areas using silk floss. 'Voiding' is a technique often used in Chinese embroidery – spaces are used to separate petals in flowers; often this is combined with gold thread.

Motifs in Chinese embroidery are highly symbolic and are often found on court robes – popular motifs include clouds, bats, butterflies and good luck symbols. Animals appeared frequently, particularly the dragon, and birds such as peacocks, pheasants and geese. Birds were embroidered in positions facing the

Dragon court robe, China 19th century

Detail

sun (representing the Emperor) along with clouds, rocks and water. The bat motif was often used, representing *fu* (good luck) – the character for happiness is also pronounced '*fu*'. These symbols were often worked in polycoloured silk, on silk or gauze backing. Chinese embroideries also featured the swastika (an ancient symbol of luck), and flowers such as lotus, peony, chrysanthemum, magnolia, cherry blossom and orchids.

Court robes of the Manchu dynasty demonstrate some of the most exquisite embroidery in China. The Manchu people took power in the 17th century and the fact that both Manchu men and women were skilled and enthusiastic riders is reflected in the altered designs of robes at this time; horse-hoof cuffs were introduced to enable the rider to hold the reins and protect their hands at the same time. The robe featured opposite is a man's court robe. The design represents the Chinese concept of universal order, and the dragon in the centre is the ancient symbol of imperial power. Embroidered stripes symbolise the sea and the image on the centre front symbolises the mountains of the earth. The dragon's head is embroidered in concentric circles using couched gold threads.

India and Pakistan

Gold is valued throughout the world, and has been associated with the divine by many cultures. Hindus believe gold was created by the fire god Agni. India has produced a number of textile styles incorporating goldwork, which has been fashionable for many centuries and is still used to decorate fashion items, particularly those associated with special occasions, and for eveningwear. Metal-thread embroidery is used to decorate the borders of clothes like this velvet jacket from Pakistan (below) which dates from the 1930s.

Embroidered velvet jacket, Pakistan, 1930s

Chinai work sari borders

Chinai work (above) was originally embroidered by Chinese embroiderers living in Gujerat, India – often the motifs and the techniques themselves demonstrate Chinese influences. Fine floss silk is used to decorate shawls, saris and children's clothing. Frequent motifs include birds and flowers, often embroidered in white on a coloured silk background.

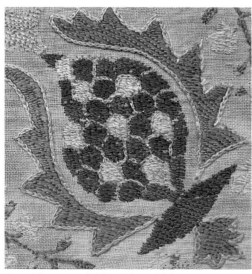

Suzani fragment, Bokhara, Central Asia

Central Asia

In Iran, Afghanistan and Turkestan many fine *suzanis* are produced. *Suzani* embroideries are named from the Persian word for 'needle'. These textiles, traditionally made for dowries, were worked on silk or linen backgrounds. Traditionally they were made as bedcovers, tablecloths and cushions, and incorporated distinctive motifs such as flowers, palmettes, leaves, and fruits such as the pomegranate (an ancient symbol of fertility).

Europe

Hand embroidery has been produced for centuries, probably the most famous is Bayeux Tapestry which was made in the 1070s. The tapestry was believed to have been commissioned by Bishop Odo of Bayeux, the half-brother of William the Conquerer. It documents the history of the Battle of Hastings, and the Norman Conquest. The Bayeux Tapestery is really an embroidery, stitched in woollen yarns on linen, using mostly stem-stitch and couching.

Between the 13th century and about 1500, England became famous for *Opus Anglicanum* (English work). This was the finest period in English embroidery and consisted of costly embroidery, usually worked by men, stitched with silk thread onto a linen cloth. This style, which consumed large quantities of silver and silver gilt thread, was used to produce fine embroideries for church vestments and the work was highly prized by monarchs and churchmen. Much of the embroidery consisted of couching, caught onto the surface of the fabric with tiny stitches. During the second half of the 14th century, opulent velvet became a popular fabric for backing embroidery. Some examples may still be seen in the Victoria and Albert Museum in London today.

Domestic embroidery was hugely popular in the 16th and 17th centuries. Embroidery and *appliqué* was used for hangings that decorated the walls of palaces and great country houses as well as domestic furnishings. Flowers and fruits, together with birds and small animals of the sort found in Elizabethan gardens, were regularly embroidered onto cushions and pillowcases.

Embroidery was also used to decorate clothing. In the 17th and 18th centuries, the most formal and costly evening shoes and gowns were lavishly decorated with couched or raised silver threads, designed to sparkle in candle-light. Much of the metal in many historic examples has now tarnished and lost its sparkle, but ornate work can still be seen.

By the 17th and 18th centuries the East India Company, originally set up to bring back spices from the East, returned to England with firstly cotton and then later silk, and these materials had a great impact on textile design. One very distinctive style of decoration in both weaving and embroidery that really characterised much of the 19th century was the introduction of the popular Paisley shawls, inspired by the shawls of Kashmir.

The word 'shawl' derives from the Persian word *shal*, which really means a type of woven fabric. This shawl industry grew in Kashmir from the 16th century and in the late 17th century these warm and beautiful shawls - woven from goats hair or wool - were acquired by travellers and members of the East India Company and brought back as presents. They became immensely popular in the 19th century and were woven and embroidered in their millions throughout the world in Persia, India, Kashmir, Russia, USA and Europe.

By about 1800 the *boteh*, which is the stylised cone-shaped motif, was the characteristic design used on these shawls. The shape of this cone varies from small and squat to a very elongated curve. The *boteh* motif probably developed from 17th century Mughal art and may have originated as a symbol of the date palm in ancient Babylon.

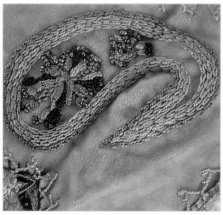

Paisley motif from 1830s shawl

Embroidery inspired from Paisley motif, 19th century

In Europe, Paisley in Scotland produced a large number of these decorated shawls, so they became known as Paisley shawls. During the 19th century, these motifs became very popular for embroidery as well as weaving.

During the latter part of the 19th century, embroidery was revived as a craft, partially in reaction to the uniform, machine-manufactured products becoming increasingly popular and available, and partially due to the influence of Art Needlework. This movement was dominated by such designers as William Morris, Walter Crane and Edward Burne Jones. A number of embroidery groups were formed and the Royal School of Art Needlework was opened in 1872. May Morris took over the art needlework embroidery at the Morris firm in 1885 and produced tablecloths, curtains and bedspreads using subtle colours such as olive green, yellows and pale turquoise. The Arts and Crafts movement greatly influenced the design of embroideries, which became simpler, more original and more stylised, influenced by other movements such as European Art Nouveau.

Embroidery in the 1920s and 1930s was influenced by Art Deco, an art movement which characteristically used large floral motifs in bold flat shapes with strong colours. Often these designs have a strongly linear quality that is easily

translated into fabric collage and *appliqué*. As they developed, the designs used simpler techniques and became freer and more abstract and experimental with more emphasis on rhythmic lines and patterns.

1930s hand embroidery

Designing with hand embroidery stitches

Embroidery is a simple technique requiring only minimal equipment. Very simple hand embroidery, using only a few basic stitches, can be effective when applied to painted backgrounds. Simple stitches from different cultural traditions can combine to create interesting pieces of embroidery. Probably the most common basic stitches include: couching, cross stitch, satin stitch, running stitch, chain stitch and buttonhole or blanket stitch.

Needles

To start with, you will need a suitable needle; this is dependent on the type of thread used. There are a variety of needles available from craft and needlecraft suppliers. Basically, the higher the number of the needle the smaller the size. It is useful to keep a collection of needles to use with different weight threads.

• Crewel – a basic embroidery needle with a fine point and a long eye to take several strands of thread.
• Chenille – a bigger needle with a larger eye for thick threads. It has a sharp point.
• Tapestry – this has a large eye and a blunt point so that it can be inserted between the threads of the fabric without splitting them.
• Sharp - a general sewing needle with a sharp point.
• Between – a short needle with a sharp point often used for quilting.
• Beading – a very fine long needle with a tiny eye so that it can go through small beads.

You will also need small embroidery scissors with sharp points as well as larger ones for cutting fabric.

Hand embroidered samples inspired by 1930s embroidery

Threads

There is now a huge variety of threads that can be used for embroidery but below are a few of the most easily available:

- Pearl cotton – twisted thread with slight sheen that can be purchased in different thicknesses.
- Cotton a broder – lightly twisted thread with a sheen.
- Soft embroidery – matt thread which comes in six strands.
- Fancy yarns – such as metallic threads.
- Sewing threads – cotton, linen or silk.

Simple stitches

Here are just a few simple and traditional embroidery stitches that can be used to enhance the surface of your textile pieces.

Couching

Couching is a way of laying down an interesting and possibly expensive thread, by attaching it to the background fabric with small stitches to hold it in place; it is often used to outline a particular shape. It was traditionally used to display threads that were too valuable to be worked into the fabric. Gold or metal thread was laid down on the surface of the fabric, then it was stitched into position with a more supple thread (see embroidered velvet jacket from Pakistan, p.61).

Couching was also used extensively in Europe in medieval church vestments that incorporated real gold imported from the East. Couching was used to make outlines for filled motifs and has been used frequently in appliqué work.

Couching is done by making a secure knot in the couching thread and laying the thread to be couched on the surface of the fabric. Make the first stitch across the end of this laid thread then make evenly spaced couching stitches to

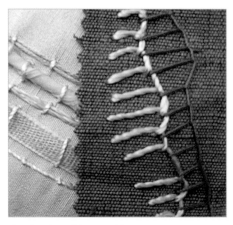

Hand and machine couching

Couching and blanket stitch

Satin stitch silk embroidery on silk, China   English satin stitch embroidery 19th century

the end of the row of laid thread. It can be very effective if you use a different thickness of thread or braid to couch onto the surface of the fabric.

Couching by machine gives you an opportunity to use a selection of different stitches to couch down the laid thread or braid. When you use a contrasting thread to couch down the laid thread, the stitches form their own patterns and can be regular or widely spaced depending on the effect that you want.

Satin stitch

Satin stitch is another simple stitch in which embroidery threads are laid down in straight flat lines to cover whole areas of the surface of textiles. It is used as a filling stitch in many cultures, and in Chinese embroidery. It was popular in Europe and was often used to define precise shapes of motifs such as leaves and flowers in Victorian silk embroideries. Satin stitch can be used to cover specific areas of quilts or embroideries to enhance the surface effect.

Cross stitch

Cross stitch is a very popular and simple way of covering a textile surface. It can be used to decoratively enhance the background surface, to make geometric patterns, or to cover the whole surface. Also, cross stitch may be sewn very finely to create a raised textural surface and to bring out specific motifs in sharp relief.

Hand embroidery sample

Chain and satin stitch

Chain stitch

This stitch has been used extensively in India, Turkey, Iran and in Europe, particularly France in the 18th century. It is often used to outline circles and combined with tiny mirrors as in India, or worked in circles as a filling stitch. Traditionally in India, chain stitch was worked with a hook called an *ari*. Ari work is the equivalent of the *tambour* work familiar to English embroiderers.

Designs with twisting and flowing lines can be very effective in chain stitch. It has been used extensively on this blouse front from Sindh, Pakistan (below, right). This style is *pakkoh* embroidery, which consists of chain stitch, satin stitch and buttonhole stitch combined with small mirrors.

Blanket or Buttonhole stitch

Buttonhole stitch is a natural border stitch often used to decorate the edges of collars and cuffs, and can be used to fasten down other fabrics securely.

Running stitch

Running stitch is a very simple stitch which forms the basis of quilting and is the characteristic stitch found on *kanthas*. See Chapter 6 for more information.

Chain-stitched bag, Northern India

Chain-stitched blouse front, Pakistan

The textile artist Diana Shone demonstrates a very subtle use of hand stitching when she uses chain stitch to edge the ends of scarves. Diana is inspired by the landscapes of the northwest of England as well as the delicacy of Indian silks and suzanis; she uses hand embroidery on the delicate hand-dyed silk mousseline scarves she produces.

Hand-embroidered shoe. Libby Smith produces exquisite and exuberant hand embroidered bags and shoes which combine the traditional hand stitches and motifs from India, Pakistan and Northern Thailand with beads and sequins.

Mixing hand and machine embroidery

Detail: machine-embroidered dyed silk quilt

Machine embroidery

These days, machine embroidery is used by most cultures to embellish and decorate the surfaces of fabrics for fashion and furnishing. The speed of the machine and the ease and versatility with automatic machine patterns and the possibilities of computer-aided design make it an attractive option. There are many books now on designing for embroidery with the use of a computer but here I will concentrate on the simple techniques of machine embroidery; these are accessible to anyone with a sewing machine with a swing needle.

Machine embroidery has given us scope to use our own unique way of inter-preting designs, patterns and motifs. It can be used just to add texture and interest to simple painted landscapes.

Using a domestic sewing machine

As long as you can lower the feed teeth (which normally move the fabric under the presser foot) you can use your machine for free embroidery. A darning foot, which comes as an attachment to your machine, can be used if you prefer not to use the needle on its own. Ideally your machine should have a zigzag facility.

Backing your work

Most fabrics can be used for machine embroidery as long as they are not too thick. Often fabrics will need some kind of backing like iron-on Vilene™ or, if they are very thin, they will need to be used with one of the vanishing fabrics such as the water soluble plastics. See p.73 for more information.

Frame

To keep lighter and medium-weight fabrics taut for machine embroidery, use an embroidery frame made of plastic, metal or wood. If using a conventional wooden embroidery hoop, bind the inner ring with bias binding to prevent the fabric from slipping. Heavier fabrics won't require a frame.

Threads

There is a huge selection of sewing threads that can be used for machine embroidery. Machine embroidery threads come in a range of weights, 30 and 40 are the most common but you can use thread as fine as 60. You can use viscose, polyester, cotton or metallic threads.

Guterman Sew All™ threads are good for beginners. These threads are strong and smooth, yet fine and knot-free. They are made from 100% polyester, will not fade, and are available in many colours including fluorescent. Madeira® sell shiny metallic threads such as gold, copper and silver and variegated metallic threads which allow interesting and unexpected colour changes. Oliver Twists® sell a range of random-dyed silk machine threads.

If you use thicker threads on the bobbin underneath, and a looser tension than normal, some of the thicker thread will appear on the surface of the fabric. You can also use thicker threads on the spool, but you may have to use a larger needle (such as a 100) to sew this thread into the fabric. Experiment on small pieces of fabric to get the effect that you want.

Instructions:
- If your fabric is light or medium-weight place it in a frame to keep it taut.
- Use an embroidery foot or remove the foot.
- Lower the teeth so that the fabric is free to move in any direction   ideally use a darning foot to protect your fingers.
- Set the tension for ordinary machine sewing.
- Put stitch length on zero.
- Bring the bottom thread up into the surface of the fabric and hold this down when you start sewing to prevent the threads being caught up.

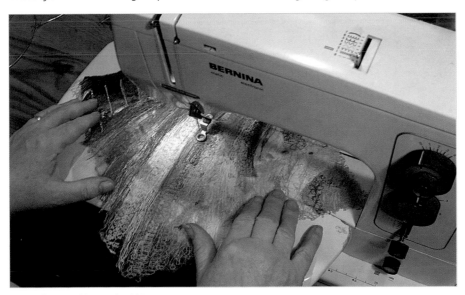

Controlling machine embroidery

• Experiment with other stitches, such as zigzag or any other variations you have on your machine, to combine with free machining.

• If you want the bobbin thread to show on the surface, tighten the top thread tension and use a contrasting thread on the bobbin. When you have mastered this technique of free stitching you can draw outlines on the fabric and machine within the shapes.

• You will need to practice controlling the speed in order to use the machine as a fine pen. Always machine steadily or you will break your needles. Control the movement of the fabric with your hands. Slow movement will produce shorter stitches and faster movements will lengthen the stitch. To fill in an area work up and down and side to side.

Useful tips:

• Use a piece of wood under the machine to tip it towards you, so you can see your work more clearly.

• Use spray starch on limp fabric to stiffen it and make sewing easier. This is useful for silk organza, lightweight jap silk, chiffon or mousseline.

• To further enhance your machine embroidery skills, experiment with a number of special effects such as using a wing needle for edges on silk and organza – the wing needle should be included in the box of sewing machine attachments for your machine. If you use a zigzag stitch, the wing needle should turn back on itself to form patterns.

• Couch down interesting threads of all thicknesses onto the surface of your embroidery by using zigzag or another decorative stitch – when couching hold the thread up for more control.

• Incorporate wire into your embroidery, couching it for a raised effect.

Machined sample on silk and felt

Water-soluble fabrics

You will often need a firm base for your machine embroidery that can be discarded when the machining has been finished. This is especially important when you are using delicate fabrics such as finer weights of silk – jap, organza or mousseline. There are a number of different types of vanishing fabric that you can buy to give initial support to your fabric; these can be either cold-water or hot-water dissolvable. The muslin-type hot-water dissolvable fabric leaves the embroidery softer than the plastic cold-water dissolvable, but you will have to experiment to see what suits you best.

Lace-edged silk velvet. For this piece, Norma Hopkins used water soluble dissolvable plastic to create lace-like edges. She sprayed and painted the background, and applied dye with syringes. She decorated the fabric with sections of devoré, then hand and machine embroidered in contrasting colours.

Machine embroidery can be produced either flat or three-dimensional, according to the type of base used. Three dimensional objects such as bowls and vases can be created, as well as jewellery, using the heavier-weight cold-water dissolvable plastic. These fabrics are very versatile as they can be used without an embroidery hoop, which can restrict the area you can work on at any one time.

Embroidered silk jacket with handmade buttons. Terri Jones is an embroiderer who produces delicate surfaces by combining machine embroidery with overlaid hand-dyed transparent fabrics. She uses free embroidery as well as automatic pattern stitches from her machine.

SIX

Other Decorative Techniques

Slashing

The practice of revealing underlayers of fabric through the top fabric dates back to the 15th century, when it was an especially popular technique for decorating men's doublets. The technique is known as 'slashing'. It was a way to enhance the opulence of clothing, by displaying as many luxury fabrics on one garment as possible. Combinations of silks, satins and rich velvets, as well as leather and suede, appeared right up to the beginning of the 17th century. Decorative motifs were sometimes stamped onto silk satins, and the material was then perforated with tiny decorative holes. Traditionally, the top fabric, usually velvet, was often pulled back and fixed with decorative ties or beads to better display the fabric underneath, and for added effect.

Slashing is particularly effective for contrasting fabrics such as silk and velvet but it can also be an interesting way of combining sheer fabrics.

Instructions:
• Machine two layers of textiles together either in strips or in a specific design.
• Cut back with sharp scissors to reveal the fabric underneath.
• The underneath fabric can be bunched up slightly, through the slashed areas, for greater effect. See the velvet jacket made by Terri Jones (below, left) which was inspired by 16th-century doublets.

Back of slashed velvet jacket by Terri Jones   Silk slashed samples

Quilted silks inspired by ikats. The design was first planned on paper and the silk material for the shapes was backed with Bondaweb™, then the pattern was cut out and ironed directly onto the background fabric. The whole pieces were then quilted over with machine stitching, which gives stability to the silk and prevents the raw edges from fraying.

Quilting

A quilt comprises two layers of fabric with a soft padding sandwiched in between. The word 'quilt' comes from the Latin *culcit* which means 'mattress filled with soft wool or feathers'. During the medieval period quilting was used for protective vests worn under heavy armour. In the 18th century garments were quilted for warmth, including women's petticoats, caps and cloaks and men's waistcoats.

Most modern quilting is done with polyester wadding, which is sold in various weights. A fabric called heirloom batting, which is 80% cotton, can also be used as the middle layer. Small running stitches can be used for hand quilting. Ordinary sewing thread may be used, but many specialist craft shops sell stronger threads, made from either polyester or linen, specifically for quilting. Many contemporary designers produce quilts which are both hand and machine quilted as well as pieced.

Appliqué

Appliqué is about cutting shapes from one fabric and using them to decorate the surface of another fabric. Although complex shapes can be applied in this way, special care must be taken to maintain corners and sharp points.

Appliqué can be machined or done by hand, depending on the technique you prefer. Most fabrics will be suitable for most techniques, but only lightweight fabrics can be used for turned-edge *appliqué*. Traditional *appliqué* was made by turning the edges of the fabric to prevent fraying.

Turned-edge *appliqué*

Instructions:

- Cut out pieces, including a seam allowance of 6–12 mm (½-⅝ in.).
- Apply iron-on interfacing to the reverse side of each piece.
- Turn over, so the piece is right-side-up, and tack down the edges by folding under the seam allowance (6-12mm).
- Stretch the background fabric over the embroidery frame.
- Pin and tack each shape into place.
- Slipstitch along the edge of each piece.
- Use a hand stitch – such as cretan stitch, feather stitch or buttonhole stitch – to decorate the edge.

Machine *appliqué* with machine edging

Instructions:

- Cut out pieces, including a seam allowance of 6–12 mm (½-⅝ in.).
- Apply iron-fusible interfacing to bond the reverse side of the fabric pieces.
- Stretch background fabric over a frame if necessary to keep it taut.
- Position your fabric pieces on the backing, in the required position. Pin and tack in place.
- Machine around the edge of each shape, using straight stitch, zigzag or another decorative automatic machine stitch of your choice. A couched thread around the edge can be effective whether sewn by hand or by machine.
- Remove tacking.

Appliqué wallhanging, Margo Singer. The velvet was hand dyed then applied to both the felt and the velvet background by hand stitching, with machining over the motifs.

Machine embroidered patchwork, Terri Jones. The silk was cut up and reassembled, then stitched over with a combination of free machine stitching and automatic machine patterns.

Bonding and *appliqué*

Combining different fabrics together by stitching, patchwork, *appliqué* or bonding can produce some exciting textures and contrasts.

To stick one fabric onto the surface of another fabric, use an iron-on fabric interfacing called Bondaweb™ or Heat bond™. These are iron-on adhesives with a sticky glue on either surface protected by peel-off paper coating. They are usually sold in sheets, but you may occasionally find it on a roll, which is useful for large projects. There are two thicknesses of Bondaweb™ available – lightweight and heavyweight. Which you choose will of course depend on the weight of the fabric. These are machine washable when applied to the backing fabric, although it is best to secure the edges by stitching if you are making clothes.

Instructions:

• Heat your iron on silk setting. Place the Bondaweb™ paper-side-up on the wrong side of the fabric piece, and iron for only 1–2 seconds.
• Allow the material to cool, then peel off the paper backing. You are left with a glue-like substance which wants to stick to another piece of fabric. The adhesive should appear milky-white in colour. If it is shiny it has been over-heated and will not stick as well.
• Position the material on the right side of the backing fabric, right-side up, where you want it to stick, and iron it gently for 3–5 seconds. This should fix it in place.

For small areas of fabric, there are a number of fabric glues that can be used. Some fabric glues are even sold in decorative colours, including gold and silver, which can be used as featured lines and decorative elements in the design.

Reverse *appliqué*

To make reverse *appliqué*, place layers of fabric on top of a base fabric. Then gradually cut away the top layer to reveal the fabric underneath. This is most effective when the layers are made of different fabrics.

Reverse *appliqué* can make use of many different fabrics. Some simple and effective samples can be made with strongly contrasting textiles such as silk, leather, metallic fabrics and felt.

Recycling

Combining patchwork, *appliqué* and quilting with recycled fabrics

In countries where fabrics can be expensive, pieces of clothing are often cut up and recycled to make new garments or bedding. Recycling makes good common sense, as it helps to avoid waste and to foster responsible attitudes towards the world's increasingly scarce resources. Re-using pre-loved fabrics is also a creative and satisfying method for making new and innovative clothes and textiles.

India

In India, *kantha* work is a good example of the textile-recycling tradition. The *kantha* style of embroidered quilt originated in West Bengal. The word 'kantha' means 'patched cloth' and women made these pieces at home out of layers of old saris and *dhotis*. These re-used textiles were stitched together, often embellished with embroidery. *Kanthas* are used for quilts, wraps for babies, pillows, cushion covers and bags.

A typical *kantha* consists of five or six layers of fabric stitched together and is embroidered, often using colourful threads unpicked from sari borders. The top layer contrasts with the colourful needlework, and is usually white; in Bengal

Kantha cloth – India

white is the traditional colour of saris and *dhotis*. The eight-petalled lotus flower often features in the centre of *kanthas* (see opposite page).

Recycling in your own work

Recycle old materials to add to your silk and velvet pieces collection. In most charity shops you will find inexpensive but interesting materials used for old dresses, tops, coats and sweaters. You can often get silk and velvet items as well as lace and interesting glitzy fabrics at affordable prices, which you can then recycle into imaginative textiles and garments.

Try combining different fabrics, such as suede and leather, to add to the textural contrast. The additional bonus of working with lightweight suede and leather is that you do not have to be concerned with turning the edges as you would with more fragile fabrics.

In many cities there are recycling projects for educational and/or craft purposes. These are an excellent source of many types of fabrics and papers. Sometimes specialist foil which has been discarded by graphic designers (and is therefore relatively inexpensive) can be found through these recycling projects.

Silk jacket made from recycled materials. Lauren Shanley is committed to recycling. She transforms vintage fabrics into collages for clothing and interiors. Her work is hand- and machine-stitched, embroidered and appliquéd and beaded into layers of colour and texture to make a range of textiles from wedding dresses to wall pieces.

Mixed media

Combine fabrics creatively – mixing the different textures and surfaces of a range of fabrics, and combining them to make innovative textile pieces. Potential fabrics are really only limited by your own imagination; to start with try a wide range of materials, from silk, velvet, voile, metallic fabrics, felt, leather and suede, to paper and foil.

As well as combining bits of recycled fabrics to add interest to the surface of your textiles, you can make your own fabrics to add to your stock. These can be incorporated into your textile designs. Two relatively simple ways of creating 'textiles' are bonding fibres to form silk papers and bonding wool to make felt. These fabrics can then be cut up and re-applied to any textile surface.

Although textile craft suppliers do sell silk paper, which can be dyed with textile dyes and paints, you can also create your own.

Making silk paper

Silk paper is made from silk fibres placed on top of each other in overlapping layers. They are then bonded together with a water-soluble glue.

You will need:
• Newspapers and plastic sheeting.
• Large paintbrush.
• A piece of net twice the size of the silk piece you want to make.
• Silk tops (natural or dyed).
• Throwsters waste – a textured, lustrous silk filament which is dyed silk or silk noils. You should be able to buy this from specialist craft suppliers.
• Cocoon strippings. These can be bought undyed so you can colour them as you choose.
• Squares of mawata caps (these are made from degummed cocoons).

All these can be made into silk paper using a silk paper medium – a water-soluble gum. You can buy it in small jars from textile suppliers, then dilute it with cold water; one part medium to eight parts water. The medium is similar to wallpaper paste, but it does not contain fungicide.

Instructions:
• Cover your work surface with plastic sheeting. Lay out a piece of net (a little larger than the piece of silk paper you want to make) on top of the plastic sheeting.
• Tease out the silk fibres you want to use and place these in a thin layer on the piece of net; the fibres should run in the same direction. Cover most of the surface of the net in a square shape.
• Tease out more fibres of silk, then lay another thin layer of fibres on top of the existing layer in another direction, overlapping the exisiting layer. This is the same process used to felt wool.
• At this stage you can place seeds or tiny pieces of silk or fancy threads on top of these layers to make interesting textures.
• Use a 2.5 cm (1 in.) brush to paint the diluted silk-paper medium over the silk fibres, making sure that the surface of the fibres is evenly coated.
• Turn the fibre-sheet over and paint the other side.
• Cover with another layer of netting to hold the fibres in place.
• Leave to dry naturally, or use a hairdryer to speed up the process.
• When dry, you can peel the netting away from both sides of the paper and peel the bonded silk fibres away from the plastic sheeting.

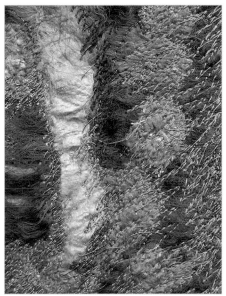 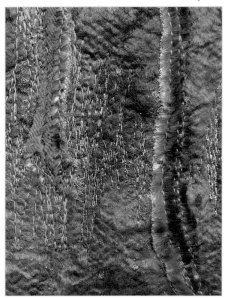

Silk paper with machine embroidery

You will now have a thin sheet of 'silk paper' which can be used with felt or other textile materials, or cut up and used for collage, or embroidered. If it is made into thick enough pieces, it can then be moulded and shaped into objects such as bowls or jewellery. Silk paper can be used on its own or it can be felted into wool felt.

Needlefelting

There are too many ways of making felt to describe here and there are many books specifically on the craft of feltmaking. However, needlefelting is a quick and useful method which can be carried out without even soap and water. This process allows you a lot of control over the design or motif that you are felting. You simply use a felting needle to jab and poke in and out of the layers of carded wool; this makes them stick together. This can be a useful method for creating small motifs to apply to other fabrics or incorporate into larger designs.

You will need:

• Carded wool (combed tops), which is sold from feltmaking suppliers in a wide range of colours. Alternatively, you could dye your own wool after carding it from the fleece; wool dyes well in acid dyes.
• Felting needles. These are sold in different sizes, depending on the delicacy of the work, and look like a crochet hook but are thinner with a prong on the end. They are used to hook through the fibres to intertwine them to form a loose felt.
• A pre-felted base to work on. You can make this, or you can buy ready-felted pieces in a range of colours from some felt suppliers or craft stores. Make your own design by cutting out shapes and collaging them back onto small pieces of

Needlefelting example inspired by rug from Iran

pre-felt; insert the needle up and down into the background layer of felt until the fibres have adhered to each other.

Lines and border patterns

Instructions:

• Take a wad of carded wool in the left hand and, using the right hand, pull a few fibres out, rubbing them thoroughly between your fingers.
• Repeat this process until you have made a continuous thin strip about 40 cm (16in.) long. This is the same technique as that used by nomads for making strings to form borders for felt carpets.
• Lay this strip onto an area of pre-felt and needle it (jabbing and poking with a needle) through the layers a few times so that it lies flat. Be careful of your fingers. The needle does not have to pass all the way through the wool, just in to a depth of about halfway, then out again. See photo above for how to hold the needle.
• Densely needle all the way along the strip, making sure it bonds well with the layer of felt underneath. This light bonding will not be as hardwearing as felt that has been rolled, but it is a useful surface on which to stitch, or to cut up and apply to other fabrics. It contrasts beautifully with silk or velvet.

Although a traditional motif has been used in the needlefelting example above, this technique offers great possibilities for making pictorial work using your own images and symbols.

Combining silk and silk paper with felt

You can add silk pieces and silk paper to felt to create fabrics with interesting surface contrasts. The silk must be lightweight; silk chiffon adds interest and texture whereas jap silk or silk satin adds luminosity to the piece. The silk and velvet pieces add an unexpected, contrasting luster to the duller surface of the wool felt.

Instructions:
• Make felt in the usual way by laying out the wet carded wool in layers on the plastic sheets.
• Place the silk pieces and small pieces of silk paper in position on the surface.
• Place a piece of net on top of the silk.

Felt jacket with silk and velvet, Lizzie Houghton

• Use a little extra soap to gently rub the paper or silk, until it sticks to the wool.
• Roll the felted piece several times, until you feel that the silk is attached firmly.
• Remove the net and roll the felt until you feel it is the thickness and density you require.

Foiling

Metallic foils add sparkle and a touch of the exotic to your fabrics. Foil can be bonded onto the surface of the fabric with glue or Bondaweb®. Most fabrics are suitable for foiling, as long as they have a smooth surface. Foiling adds surface interest, and is versatile as it is available in many metallic colours.

Sheet foil on a cellophane backing is available from many craft suppliers. It is expensive, but even a small amount can be very effective; its jewel-like metallic sheen can really enhance the surface quality of your textiles. You could also try using gold-coated gift

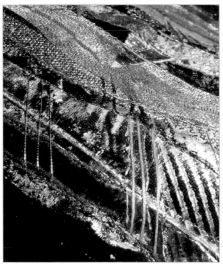

Pink and turquoise foiled piece

Red foiled piece stencilled and machine stitched

paper; when foiled, the colour will be a kind of antique silver. These foiled papers do not bond as well as the foil sold by craft suppliers in packs, but they can be used to create interesting fragmented and antiqued looks. Packs of small squares are a good way to experiment when starting out, as foil can be expensive.

Decorative foils can be applied to a variety of fabrics such as velvet, silk, cotton, synthetic fabrics and suede. Fleece and wool fabrics can also be foiled but this will result in blurred shapes; smooth surfaces work best. Foils come in a selection of dazzling colours and are machine washable when fixed to the surface of the fabric.

There are various ways of applying foil to the surface of the fabric. If using fabric glue, which has a rubbery texture, allow it to dry before gently ironing on the foil, using a low iron setting. Fabric glues come in transparent shades or in metallic colours, and these can be used to add more decoration to your design. Alternatively, you can use Bondaweb®, Heatbond® or Wonderweb®, available in packets or on the roll from craft suppliers and sometimes in department stores.

Instructions:
• Choose fabrics with a smooth surface for foiling.
• Use a small square of cotton, silk or velvet, and place onto a slightly padded surface such as an old towel covered with plastic sheeting.
• Apply fabric glue, using a sponge, to a wooden block or rubber stamp. Make sure that the glue is dry before using the foil - you can use a hairdryer to speed up the drying process.
• Once dried, press the foil on by hand or lightly iron it with the shiny side upward. NB: Do not iron directly onto the foil; it must be covered with a sheet of thin paper.
• Foil can be re-used until very little colour remains on the cellophane. You can also use certain glue pens for lettering or for more fine detail as in a drawing.

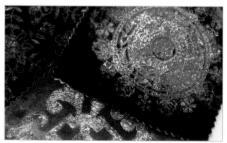

Antiqued effect foiled pieces

Foiling with applied layers of fabric

Fix velvet fragments on top of the Bondaweb on velvet

Place thin foil across the entire area

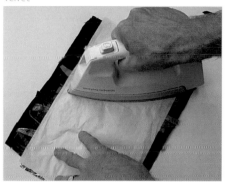

Cover with paper backing, then iron over foil

First foiling

Foiling with velvet

Foil can also be used to cover a whole area, using Bondaweb® or Heatbond® to stick the foil to the background fabric.

Instructions:
- Cut the foil to the size and shape required.
- Place the adhesive-side-down on the backing fabric.
- Cover with thin paper, and iron using a silk setting. It is important to only iron for 4–6 seconds, as overheating will ruin the bond.
- When the adhesive is bonded to the background fabric, it will be a milky white colour. Press the pieces of velvet down firmly, where you want them to sit.
- Cover the foil with a sheet of paper and iron over again for just a few seconds at the same heat setting.
- Peel the foil off. It will only have stuck in the areas where it is exposed to the adhesive.
- Several areas of foiling can be built up in this way until the desired effect is achieved. If you want to add more foil or make marks across the design, use fabric glue to apply more foil in the desired positions.

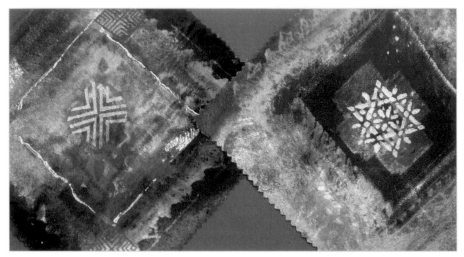

Squares decorated using glue pens and foil

Experimenting

• Foiling can be effectively combined with stamping, stencilling and machine and hand stitching.

• Linear foiling can be used to give directional emphasis to a piece.

• Experiment with using a glue pen when foiling, to enhance and pick out specific areas of a design.

• Try sponging fabric glue onto the surface of stamps or apply it with a brush through a stencil. All these must be washed immediately after use to get rid of the glue. This can give a muted and subtle antiqued effect.

• Foiling combines well with *appliqué* velvet and silk. Try couching the edges of the silk and velvet with metallic threads and stamping the whole surface using wooden blocks.

Directional foiling with hand and machine stitching

SEVEN

Making Accessories and Gifts

As well as using silk and velvet for fashion and clothing you can make a wide range of accessories using these versatile materials on their own, or mixing them with other textile techniques.

Bags

Bags are a good starting point for textiles as they require very little material, are relatively easy to make and can be made out of a range of materials.

Three foiled bags made from recycled strips of silk and velvet. These have been glued to a backing, then metallic foil added to enhance the surface.

Foiled bags

Instructions:
• Decide what shape you want your bag to be. The three bags illustrated here are the simplest shapes, as they just consist of a front and a back with attached separate straps. The bags featured overleaf are also simple shapes and are made up of only three pieces – front, back and a side piece made from silk which joins both front and back and is the same length as both pieces. These shapes allow a bit more room in the bag.
• Experiment with cutting out templates for your bags from pieces of newspaper or thin paper. When you have decided on a shape, make a paper pattern or a thin card template, remembering to add seam allowances of 1.5 cm (⅝ in.) all round. Remember also to allow enough for the base of the bag.
• Cut a template for the side piece that will join the front and back, measuring carefully to get the required shape. You may want to cut the base

Black bag with foiled pictures, Margo Singer   Ginger silk bag, Margo Singer

and sides separately.

• Measure the length of the curved edge you want, and cut out a template to fit the side of the front and back of the bag; this will be the side piece joining the front to the back. Cut this side piece from a contrasting material such as silk dupion.

• Consider the function of your bag. If it is to be used only occasionally, as a decorative evening bag for example, you will probably only need a cotton or Vilene backing as it will be lined. However if you want the bag to be stronger you should use a strong canvas material base to back the silk or velvet.

• Cut out the material for your bag and the strengthening material for the base of the bag, plus the lining.

• Press Vilene® onto the wrong side of the fabric as appropriate, depending on the weight of the material. Alternatively, you may want to stitch the fabric onto heavyweight canvas backing, if you want firm sides for your bag.

• Cut out the bag fabric, allowing a bit of extra material around the edge to make it easier to decorate. You can cut these down to actual size later.

• Mark on the front and back the actual finished size of the bag using a dressmaker's marker pen. This will allow you to see the actual shape so that you can place your fragments of fabric accurately onto the surface.

• Cut out two strips of silk for a flap if appropriate, or use your own design for fastening. Back this with Vilene®.

Bag handles

Handles for the bags featured (this page and previous page) were made from two pieces of Vilene®-backed silk dupion measuring 40 cm (16 in.).

• Fold fabric lengthways and stitch together.

• Turn inside out to form long tubes and press flat.

• Thread several strands of heavyweight knitting wool through the tubes using a bodkin – a needle with a very large eye to accommodate thick threads.

• Machine-stitch the silk pieces in the required places on the bag before the bag pieces are sewn together.

Decorating your bag

At this stage you can use foiling, stamping and decorative stitching on both the front and back of the bag.

Instructions:

• Cut the strips of velvet, silk, organza, leather or suede (or whatever decorative fabric you want to use) and place on the surface of the bag shape.
• Arrange in whatever pattern or design you want. Remember to allow some gaps in between each strip of silk or velvet, so that there is room for the foil to stick in between.
• Foil, following the instructions on p.83.
• When you have foiled the shape for the bag review the design. You can add more foil at this stage or leave the surface as it is and begin to build up interesting textures by stamping and stencilling over it.

For the bags illustrated opposite, contrasting metallic or decorative embroidery threads were placed against the edge of the fragments of velvet and couched down using a small zigzag stitch on the machine. The surface of the bags was then built up using a long machine stitch size 3 or 4. Using the quilting foot, the whole surface was then machined over in a gentle curving design. More couching with contrasting or toning threads in a variety of colours (both metallic and matt) was used to further enhance the surface of the bags. All the added stitching gives added stability and durability to the surface of the bag.

Finishing

Instructions:

• Stitch the front and back of each bag to the long side piece which is backed with medium-weight Vilene®.
• Sew all the bag pieces for the lining together once they have been lined with Vilene® for extra stiffness and strength.
• Then sew the whole bag, with right sides together, apart from the top, which should either be hemmed and the fastening attached, or sewn to your chosen flap with fastening.
• Finally, when the bag and the lining have been put together, the silk lining should be sewn into the bag using a small, tidy slipstitch.

Black silk bag, Margo Singer

Shibori velvet drawstring bag with toning silk *appliqué*

Instructions:

• Decorate your velvet using the shibori technique described in Chapter 3 (p.29).

• Cut a piece of paper (24 x 24 cm/9½ x 9½ in.) to use to make a pattern.

• Place the paper pattern onto the velvet right side up – pin, then cut to size.

• Cut out two shibori rectangles from the paper pattern for the main body of the bag. The pattern includes 1cm seam allowances.

• Fold the pattern back to a paper rectangle measuring 24 x 18 cm (9½ x 7 in.). Cut the shibori velvet to this size.

• Use tailor's chalk to mark a line 6 cm/2⅓ in. from the top of this piece; this is where the top stitched line for the casing for the drawstring will be.

• Mark another line 1.5 cm below this for the lower line of the casing stitching.

• Unfold the paper pattern, then cut an entire piece of silk for the lining.

• Cut a circle (14 cm/5½ in. diameter) of silk dupion for the bottom of the bag.

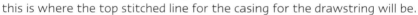

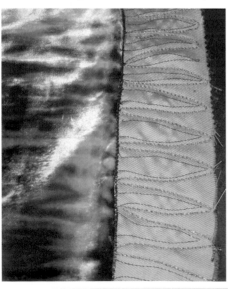

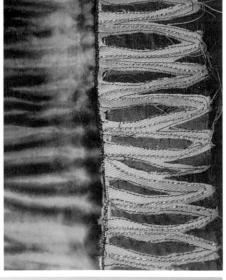

- Cut the 8-cm-wide strips for the lower section from two layers of toning silk dupion. Tack these together.
- Cut a circle shape for the lining silk.
- Iron lightweight Vilene® onto the back of the shibori velvet.
- Using a pink metallic thread, freely stitch a lozenge shape down the short end of the two layers of silk band at the base of the bag - accentuate the shapes of the velvet shibori.
- Add a metallic braid by using a narrow zigzag stitch onto the surface of the silk to further accentuate the lozenge shape.
- For the reverse *appliqué*, use very sharp scissors to cut back to the first layer of silk, trimming close to the machined lines to produce a reverse *appliqué* effect.
- With right sides together, sew the strip of silk to the bottom edge of the shibori velvet.
- Turn to right side, then press over the join. Zigzag using a contrasting metallic braid thread to pick up the pink colours of the shibori.
- Cut the circular base of the bag from silk dupion and back this with iron-on Vilene®.
- Sew the lining together. Turn right sides together and sew all but 10 cm of the top of bag.
- Sew two parallel lines at 6 and 8 cms respectively down from the top, making sure these lines are straight and match at the side seams to make a casing. Thread a piece of cord through the casing and draw the bag together.
- Press and/or hand stitch the gap between lining and outer closed. Then carefully finish it by machine stitching closely to the edge of the top of the bag.

Silk dupion and shibori velvet bag with felt and beads

Instructions:

• Cut three strips of dupion 5cm wide and lay them on a bag-sized piece of shibori velvet. Stitch these down.

• Place a length of metallic braid over the edge. Tack, machine stitch, then zigzag over, to fix it in place.

• Cut six diamond shapes from purple felt. Hand stitch these into place on top of the strips of silk (see photo above). Use a running stitch with embroidery thread to accentuate shape of diamonds.

• Hand stitch two turquoise metallic beads onto the centre of each felt diamond.

• Fold right sides together, and machine stitch a strip of dupion silk to the long edge.

• Cut out four lozenge shapes in blue felt and 4 smaller lozenge shapes in pink felt.

• Hand sew lozenges – smaller centred on top of larger – to the background fabric.

• Sew a metallic bead in the centre of each lozenge-set. Attach four small diamonds of voile between each lozenge shape. Pin or tack, then machine embroider over each diamond several times.

Lining

• Cut the lining the same size as complete bag shape, with a circle for base.

• Line the base with iron-on Vilene®.

• Sew the ends of the lining together. Turn right-side out and sew this carefully onto the base.

• Use sharp scissors to carefully trim the curves if necessary.

• Turn inside out and sew with right sides together, leaving a gap of 10cm, and turn it back right-way (shibori-side) out.

• Sew two parallel lines at 6 and 8 cms respectively down from the top, making sure these lines are straight and match at the side seams to make a casing. Thread a piece of cord through the casing and draw the bag together.

• Press and/or hand stitch the gap between lining and outer closed. Then carefully finish it by machine stitching closely to the edge of the top of the bag.

Books and boxes

Blank books can be bought very cheaply from a number of craft shops such as Hobbycraft® and can be covered to make unique yet stunning presents by covering in velvet or silk and adding foiling, stamping and stitchery.

Silk and velvet covered books

Silk boxes and bags

Silk and velvet cards

Cards

You can buy a large range of cards with different shaped inserts or you can make your own from thin card. Cards make attractive frames for decorated and stitched pieces of silk and velvet. You will only need a simple motif to make an effective appliqué card so collect ideas for these in your sketchbook.

Card templates: handmade and store-bought

Instructions:

• Take your purchased card templates, or cut out shapes for the central motifs from thin pieces of card. Make sure that these fit neatly within the cut-out area of the card templates, where they will be displayed.

• Cut two identical pieces of fabric for the inside of the cut-out card shape, measuring it about 1cm wider than the edges of the cutout. Place this fabric across each corner.

• Using tailors' chalk, mark a line with a ruler across each corner then zigzag along the line using a contrasting thread.

• Using very sharp scissors, trim the

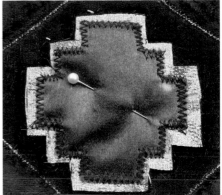

central shape back to the dark fabric (navy velvet has been used in this example) at the corners.

• Cut the shape from silk and then cut another shape only cms wider out of contrasting fabric.

• Cut a further shape from black felt (or similar) for the outer shape.

• Pin the smaller silk shape onto the larger one and tack them into place.

• Zigzag around the edge of the smaller shape with black thread.

• Straight stitch around the edge of this zigzag in metallic gold (or other contrasting) thread.

• Zigzag over the overlapping metallic thread to neaten the edges.

• Then sew a diamond shape (or other shape of your choice) in the centre of the motif. Be careful to use small stitches – this will slow you down and protect the areas you sew as they become more intricate. Sew two lines inside the diamond shape parallel to the edge.

• Carefully, with very sharp scissors, trim back the outer shape of the diamond to the metallic fabric.

• Cut the inside diamond back through two layers to the purple velvet below.

• To finish, attach double-sided tape to each side and corner inside the cover of the card. Position the embroidered card as you want it to be placed, and press down firmly. The inside of the card flap presses the embroidery onto the tape and fixes it in place.

Cushions

Although you can now buy plenty of very decorative cushions it is fun and challenging to create your own unique designs. Cushions make great gifts. They are simple to make, as there are a number of ways of fastening depending on your skill level and the kind of look you want to achieve. If you don't want to put zippers in them you can overlap the material at the back and finish with ties or buttons. If you are using silk or velvet and creating a sumptuous decorated surface on the front of the cushion, you can still choose cheaper toning fabric for the back.

Tips for making cushions:

• You can make cushions in pretty much any shape and size you want, but stick to square or rectangular shapes at first. You can then adapt this, to make more luxurious items such as roll-pillows or velvet bolsters for the bedroom.

• Consider the cushions' function before you choose your fabric and decorative methods. Does it need to be hardwearing, i.e., will it be used as a floor cushion, are there pets and children around? Or will it be purely decorative? For a cushion that will get lots of use and abuse, choose a sturdier fabric and a strong finish for your seams and fastenings. Beads and other bits that might fall off the decoration or fastening are, of course, not appropriate for a cushion that a small child might play with. Consider also whether the cushion will need to be washable.

• Consider the furnishings and colour scheme of the room the cushion will live in, and choose contrasting or toning fabrics and colours.

• If you are using a pattern or design for the cushion, remember to centralise it for best effect, so measure carefully before cutting.

• Don't skimp on zipper length. Remember, the longer the zip, the easier it will be to remove your cushion inner for cleaning or repairs, and the less risk you will run of damaging the zip-stitching or the fabric itself.

• Sewing a fabric-covered button into the centre of a round cushion will create a more padded appearance.

Silk and velvet cushions, Margo Singer

This cushion features velvet that has been stencilled and machined, with braid added to define the different areas of colour.

Making a velvet cushion

Instructions:

• For the front of the cushion: Make a rectangle of collaged and foiled velvet measuring 18 x 22 cm (7 x 8½ in.).
• Make a border for this rectangle by sewing, with right sides together, four strips of silk, each 4 cm (1½ in.) wide, around all four sides.
• Turn the fabric over, press and machine closely around the edge to flatten the silk.
• Cut two strips of turquoise silk dupion 15 x 10 cm (6 x 4 in.). Sew these strips either side of a 6 cm (2½ in.) strip of lurex covered with a layer of blue voile, right sides together.
• Press and turn out.
• On either side of this complete strip, sew a strip of dark blue velvet measuring 12 cm (5 in.) wide.
• Place the large square of vevet fragments plus the silk border on top of the velvet, pin, tack and machine stitch into place.
• Sew the braid around each edge of this central square, overlapping by 4 cm (1½ in.) on the corners.
• For the back of cushion: Place together two rectangles of velvet overlapping by 12 cms (5 in.).
• Pin these with right sides together, then machine around the complete edge of the cushion leaving a 1 cm (½ in.) seam.
• Turn inside out and place the cushion pad inside the cushion cover to finish the cushion.

The diamond pieces were pinned and tacked on top of a turquoise silk strip. This silk strip was tacked and then machined onto the backing velvet.

Silk and velvet wallhanging

The design for this wallhanging emerged after experimenting with crayons and felt-tip pens. The materials used were silk dupion and metallics, and the backing is a dark blue velvet with a vertical watermarked pattern. The velvet was backed with lightweight, iron-on Vilene®.

Strips of velvet were used as a collage, placed onto Bondaweb®, then foiled and stamped over in a random pattern, using stamps made from corrugated card and a stencil made from sequin waste. The silk and velvet strip was then cut to make the five applied diamond shapes, and braid or decorative ribbon was used to accentuate the edges.

To hang the piece, an extra section of velvet measuring 25 x 62 cm (10 x 25 in.) was hemmed and then attached to the top of the hanging. This was left open at both ends, to allow a piece of dowelling or pole to be inserted. This blue silk band could also be quilted, using random stitching and a toning thread. This will give a soft, dimpled effect.

Backing was made from a strong cotton in a toning colour. The wallhanging was pinned to the backing, and the backing trimmed 2 cm (¾ in.) wider all around. The overlap was then wrapped around to the front, pressed, then carefully handsewn into place. This made a border to finish the hanging.

EIGHT

Inspiration, Planning and Development

This chapter covers the inspiration behind the artists' work featured, and also examines how you can use your own personal source materials to develop uniquely designed textile pieces.

Design ideas can come from any number of sources – possibly the most common being the natural world, landscapes, urban cityscapes or your garden. If you sketch, record and photograph what you see that intrigues and inspires you, you will have a good starting point from which to develop your own individual style of designing.

Nature

Plants, flowers, trees, birds and animals all give you a wealth of patterns and contrasting textures. Look at the detail or from interesting angles or enlarge parts of a flower or leaf for its particular texture and pattern. If you are skilled on the computer with programs such as Adobe Photoshop®, you can manipulate your own photos to produce a range of designs for your work.

Flowers

Large leaf

Garden foliage

Begonia leaf

Architecture

Studying and developing designs from architectural features from traditional and historical buildings to modern present day buildings can be a good starting point. Churches can be a wonderful source of inspiration from the interior and ceiling, wood or stone carving and stained glass windows to the tiles on the floor.

Patterns from architectural features can come from wooden carvings on buildings such as the example of the medieval stave church just outside Bergen, Norway, or timber framed buildings such as Little Moreton Hall in Cheshire.

The lines, shapes and surfaces of modern buildings such as the Imperial War Museum and the Lowry in Salford also offer inspiration for the design of textile pieces and quilts.

Stave church Bergen, Norway

Little Moreton Hall, Cheshire

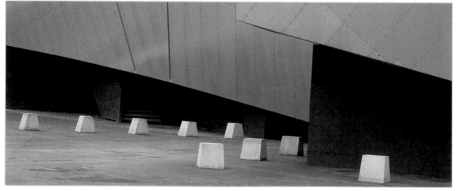
Imperial War Museum, Salford

Inspiration from other cultures

Rugs and kilims

'Kilim' is a term used to describe an oriental flat weave rug, which was traditionally produced by nomadic tribesmen from Morocco to Turkestan. These days
many rugs come from Turkey, Iran and Afghanistan. Most department stores
have collections of rugs in varied designs as well as printed ikat material in their
dress and furnishing fabric sections. These display a wealth of fascinating
symbols, which have religious or cultural meaning in the countries where these
textiles originate. The designs and colours used in carpets and rugs are usually
symbolic, as are the motifs. Many rugs have a central medallion, which may be
floral or geometric.

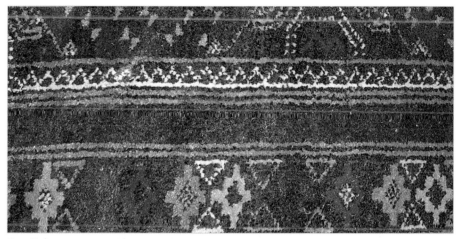

Rug, Turkey

Carpet, Iran

Rug, Iran

Hats from Afghanistan

Hats

These three skull caps (above) come from Afghanistan. The geometric cap comes from the Kandahar region of central southern Afghanistan. The quilted effect of the geometric design is achieved by close satin or buttonhole stitch over laid threads.

Kasia velvets

The Kuba people of Zaire have a long history of using elaborate patterns to decorate their architecture, carving, baskets and textiles. They produce embroidered, dyed and appliquéd raffia textiles using bold and dramatic contrasting and often very linear designs in limited colour ranges. Often flat stem-stitch embroidery is used between the areas of pile for contrast. These pieces are called 'Kasai velvets'; they resemble velvets as they have a cut-pile surface. The pile-cloths are actually made by an embroidery technique, in which raffia fibre is stitched with a needle under one warp or weft of the base cloth and then trimmed close to the front surface with a small knife. This cut embroidery stitch actually creates the carpet or velvet-like surface and their abstract linear patterns give them a very distinctive appearance.

Shoowa cut-pile raffia fabric, Zaire

Pastel sketches of motifs found in rugs   Pastels and watercolours Norma Hopkins

Developing your ideas

- Study all the relevant books and articles you can find.
- Explore your local libraries for specialist art sections and magazine collections.
- Visit textile collections in museums such as the V&A in London.
- Build up your own personal file of exciting ideas from your own photos, sketches, postcards and fabric scraps.
- Collect lots of ideas on patterns, colour and design.
- Buy a small sketchbook you can fit into your bag or pocket, and carry it everywhere, using it whenever the mood takes you. Record lots of information, saving it up for when you have time to work with it.
- Make collages by cutting up parts of your design work and rearranging them in different ways.
- Experiment with mixing different media to create different colour and texture combinations, which can be translated into textiles.
- Finally, experiment on fabric, make small samples and combine lots of different techniques and hand and machine stitching.

Transferring embroidery designs onto fabrics

If you want to transfer images, motifs or patterns from your own drawings to the surface of lightweight fabrics, the best way is to use a light box. You can buy small lightboxes from craft suppliers fairly cheaply.

Instructions:
- Place the drawing/design on top of the light box.
- Place a lightweight material, such as silk, on top of that.
- Mark the design onto the fabric with a soft pencil or a water soluble fabric marker pen.
- Alternatively, you could use dressmakers' carbon paper to transfer the design you want to the fabric by retracing the outline of the design.

Museum collections

UK

Bankfield Museum, *Halifax* - Indian, African, Indonesian, Balkan and contemporary textiles - www.calderdale.gov.uk

Bolton Museum, *Bolton* – Egyptian, Coptic- www.boltonmuseums.org.uk Palestinian and Peruvian textiles

Brighton Museum, *Brighton* – Costume

Fitzwilliam Museum, *Cambridge* - European and Oriental decorative arts - www.fitzmusem.cam.ac.uk

Gawthorpe Hall, *Padiham*– Costume, embroidery - www.nationaltrust.org.uk

Macclesfield Silk Museums, Macclesfield www.silk-macclesfield.org

Manchester Museum, Manchaster – Ethnography - www,museum.man.ac.uk

Museum of Costume, *Bath* - www.museumofcostume.co.uk

Museum of Costume, *Manchester* www.manchestergalleries.org

Museum of Science and Industry, *Manchester* - textiles gallery - www.msim.org.uk

Pitt Rivers Museum, *Oxford* - Ethnography - www.prm.ox.ac.uk

Rochdale Museum – Asian textiles

Victoria and Albert Museum, *London* – largest collection of textiles and costume in UK – www.vam.ac.uk

Whitworth Museum, *Manchester* – specialist textile collections www.whitworth.man.ac.uk

Also contact:
www.embroiderersguild.com
www.quiltersguild.org.uk
www.feltmakers.com
www.textilesociety.org.uk
www.costumesociety.org.uk

USA

Museum of Fine Art, *Boston* - textile and fashion arts - www.mfa.org

Brooklyn Museum, *New York* - decorative arts - www.brooklynmuseum.org

American Museum of Natural History, *New York* - www.amnh.org

Cooper-Hewitt Museum of Design, *New York* - historic and contemporary design - www.cooperhewitt.org

Field Museum of Natural History, *Chicago* - textiles from around the world, including Latin America and China - wwwfieldmuseum.org

Fowler Museum of Cultural History, *University of California, Los Angeles* - Ethnography - www.fowler.ucla.edu

Museum of International Folk Art, *Santa Fe* - textiles and costumes - www.moifa.org

Minneapolis Institute of Arts, *Minneapolis* - textiles from around the world, spanning 15 centuries - www.artsmia.org

The Textile Museum, *Washington* - www.textilemuseum.org

University of Pennsylvania Museum of Archaeology and Anthropology, *Philadelphia* - www.museum.upenn.edu

Collage work from Bramhall, Norma Hopkins

Suppliers

UK

Pongees (fabrics - silk, velvet, cotton)
28–30 Hoxton Square
London NI 6NN
Tel 020 7739 9130
www.pongees.co.uk

Whaleys (fabrics - silk, velvet, cotton)
www.whaleys-bradford.ltd.uk

Bennetts Silks (fabrics - silk, velvet)
www.bennett-silks.co.uk

George Weil, Fibrecrafts (dyes, paints)
Old Portsmouth Road
Peasemarsh
Surrey GU3 1LZ
www.georgeweil.co.uk

Voirrey Embroidery Centre
Brimstage Hall
Wirral L63 6JA
Tel 0151 342 3514

Rainbow Silks (embroidery supplies)
6 Wheelers Yard
Great Missenden
Bucks HP16 111
Tel 01494 862111
www.rainbowsilks.co.uk

Winifred Cottage (embroidery supplies)
17 Elms Road
Hants GU51 3EG
Tel 01252 617667
www.winifredcottage.co.uk

Stef Francis (embroidery supplies)
Waverley, Higher Rocombe
Stokeignhead, Newton Abbot
Devon TQ12 4QL
Tel 01803 323004

Kemtex Colours (dyes, paints, fabrics)
Chorley Business & Technology Centre
Euxton Lane, Chorley
Lancs PR7 6TE
www.kemtex.co.uk

Mulberry Silks (embroidery supplies)
Patricia Wood
Silkwood
4 Park Close
Telbury
Glos GL8 8HS
www.mulberrysilks-patriciawood.com

Art Van Go (embroidery supplies)
The Studios
1 Stevenage Road
Knebworth
Herts SG3 6AN
www.artvango.co.uk

USA

Thai Silks (mail order)
252F State Street, Los Altos
CA 94041-2053
www.thaisilks.com

Test Fabrics Inc (mail order)
PO Box 26
415 Delaware Avenue
West Pittston, PA 18643
Tel 001 570 603 0432
www.testfabrics.com

Jacquard Products (dyes and fabrics)
Rupert, Gibbon and Spider
PO Box 425
Healdsburg, CA 95448
Tel 001 800 442 0455
www.jacquardproducts.com

Clothilde Inc (threads)
2 Sew Smart Way B8031
Steven's Point, WI 54481 - 8031
Tel 800 722 2891

Dick Blick (art supplies, dyes)
Box 1267
Galesburg IL61402
Tel 001 800 828 4548
www.dickblick.com

Dharma Trading Co. (dyes, fabrics)
Box 150916
San Rafael, CA 94915
Tel 001 800 542 5227

Madeira USA (novelty threads)
PO Box 6068
Laconia NH 03247-6068
Tel 800 225 3001

Jonestones (foil)
33865 United Avenue
Pueblo, CO 81001
Tel 800 216 0616
www.jonestones.com

Impress Me (stamps)
www.impressmenow.com

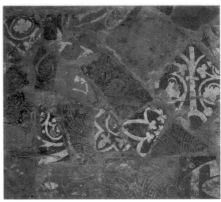
Medieval tiles

CANADA

Maiwa Handprints (dyes and fabrics)
6-1666 Johnston Street
Granville Island
Vancouver
British Columbia V6H 2SZ
Tel 011 604 669 3939
www.maiwa.com

FURTHER CONTACTS:

Jim & Diane Gaffney
www.textiletechniques.co.uk

Joanne Eddon
www.j-eddon.freeserve.co.uk

Lizzie Houghton
www.lizziehoughton.com

Maggie Relph
www.africanfabric.co.uk

Caroline Hall
www.canga.freeserve.co.uk

Sketches from tiles

Further reading

The Textile Directory – The Essential Guide to Creative Textiles – Word 4 Word (published annually)

Adler, P. & Barnard, N.; *African Majesty – Textile Art of the Ashanti and Ewe*; Thames and Hudson, 1992

Ashelford, Jane; *The Art of Dress Clothes and Society 1500-1914*; The National Trust, 1996, Baker, Patricia; *Islamic Textiles*; British Museum Press, 1995

Balfour Paul, Jenny; *Indigo*; British Museum Press, 1998

Bawden, Juliet; *The Art and Craft of Applique*; Mitchell Beazley, 1991

Beck, Thomasina; *The Embroiderers' Story – Needlework from the Renaissance to the Present Day*; David and Charles, 1995

Boscence, Susan; *Handblock Printing and Resist Dyeing*; David and Charles, 1985

Callan, A.; *Women Artists of the Arts and Crafts Movement*; Pantheon Books, 1979

Clark, Hazel; *Textile Printing*; Shire Publications, 1985

Clarke, Duncan; *The Art of African Textiles*; Grange Books, 2002

Crill, Wearden & Wilson; *Dress in Detail from Around the World*; V&A Publications, 2002

Ettinger, Rosean; *Handbags*; Shiffer Publishing Ltd. USA, 1991

Fairfield, Helen; *The Embroidery Design Sourcebook*; Cassell, 1994

Farrell, Jaqueline; *The Book of Waistcoats*; Quarto, 1991

Gillow, J. & Barnard, N.; *Traditional Indian Textiles*; Thames and Hudson, 1991

Good Housekeeping; *Step by Step Needlecraft*; Ebury Press, 1994

Guerrier, Katherine; *Quilting Masterclass*; Quarto, 2000

Guerrier, Katherine; *Patchwork and Quilting*; Batsford, 1996

Hart & North; *Historical Fashion in Detail - 17th and 18th centuries*; V&A Publishers, 2003

Kinnersley Taylor, J.; *Dyeing and Screen Printing on Textiles*; A&C Black, 2003

Lawther, Gail; *Inspirational Ideas for Embroidery on Clothes and Accessories*; Search Press, 1993

Lussier, Suzanne; *Art Deco Fashion*; V&A Publications, 2003

Morrell, Anne; *The Techniques of Indian Embroidery*; B.T. Batsford, 1992

Polakoff, Claire; *African Textiles and Dyeing Techniques*; Routledge & Kegan Paul, 1982

Robinson, Stuart; *Exploring Fabric Printing*; Studio Vista, 1970

Sandberg, Gosta; *Indigo Textiles – Techniques and History*; A&C Black, 1989

Storey, Joyce; *Manual of Textile Printing*; Thames and Hudson, 1992

Tudor, Linda; *Embroidered Purses – design and techniques*; B.T. Batsford, 2004

Waring, Lyn; *Hats Made Easy*; Sally Milner Publishing, 1995

Wells, Kate; *Fabric Dyeing and Printing*; Conran Octopus, 1997

Welsh, Nancy; *Tassels – the Fanciful Embellishment*; Lark Books, 1992

Index